THINK MEDIA SERIES:
EGS MEDIA PHILOSOPHY SERIES

The Little Book of Daesthetics:

A Fragmented Dictionary

ATROPOS PRESS
new york · dresden

Lori Martindale

The Little Book of Daesthetics:

A Fragmented Dictionary

General Editor:
Wolfgang Schirmacher

Editorial Board:
Giorgio Agamben
Pierre Alferi
Hubertus von Amelunxen
Alain Badiou
Judith Balso
Judith Butler
Diane Davis
Martin Hielscher
Geert Lovink
Larry Rickels
Avital Ronell
Michael Schmidt
Friedrich Ulfers
Victor Vitanza
Siegfried Zielinski
Slavoj Žižek

Dr. Andrew Spano, Editorial Director

Copyright © 2022 by Lori Martindale
Think Media EGS Series is supported by the European Graduate School

ATROPOS PRESS
New York • Dresden
151 First Avenue # 14, New York, N.Y. 10003
Mockritzer Str. 6, D-01219, Dresden, Germany

Cover/interior design by David/Andjela

All rights reserved.
ISBN: 978-1-7375591-1-5

"In the tradition of the philosophical poem, Lori Martindale picks through the shrapnel of aesthetics, finding scraps of a once meaningful yet abandoned yield of language mangled by the winds of forgetfulness. Swinging on the notion of the 'hinge' we see the worlds of Sappho to Cixous, Bataille and Derrida, among other MPVs, come 'unhinged,' prone to the prompts of a vertigo that creates new galaxies out of voided Being.

"[This] work skillfully elicits the innuendo of a haunted archive that hosts a house rebellion, rumbling in the background of our shared existence, when the ruckus is not front and center."

– Avital Ronell,

University Professor of the Humanities
at New York University

The Little Book of *Daesthetics*:

A Fragmented Dictionary

On daesthetics: lacunose and palimpsestic *undecidables* – *floating between finitude* - Poetry, Painting, Philosophy, and Music.

Dictionarium "collection of words or phrases" from diction "word," noun of action from past participle stem of dicere "speak, tell, say," from PIE root *deik to show, also to pronounce solemnly.

1785 Francis Grose "The Classical Dictionary of the Vulgar Tongue":

Dictionary: "a malevolent literary device for cramping the growth of a language and making it hard and inelastic. This dictionary, however, is a most useful work."

– Grose

Daesthetic[1] dictionary: a work
of wordplays, palimpsestic[2]
texts, puzzles, postponements,
musical notes, memorials,
lacunae, and elastic aporias…

---

[1] /deTH/. The state of being dead.
/es THedik/ a philosophy of art.
[2] A palimpsestic: palimpsest is a parchment
that has been inscribed and reinscribed with the
previous text being imperfectly erased and partly
visible. This concept is a metaphor for texts as
layered but sociohistorical time as imperfect
erasures where the past is partly visible in the
present.

"My heart's grown heavy, my knees will not support me/… This state I oft bemoan; but what's to do? / Not to grow old, being human, there's no way"

        - Sappho, Book IV.

> "I like the dead, they are the doorkeepers who while closing one side give way to the other."
>
>   - Cixous

Notes on Lacunae

What is Daesthetics?

Undecidable Leavings on Finitude and Art.

/deTH/. The state of being dead.
/es THedik/ a philosophy of art.

"To begin (writing, living) we must have death"

- Hélène Cixous

Prologue:

The Little Book of Daesthetics is filled with lacunae, an indeterminate[3] dictionary on the word *daesthetics*.[4] It is composed of fragmented book entries, liminal uncertainties and undecidables, art, poetry, artifacts, and philosophy.

What is Daesthetics? is not an attempt to define daesthetics as a closed definition, but rather as an open investigation into mysterious

---

[3] Open; unending.
[4] Death/Aesthetics

lacunae[5], variables of palimpsestic[6] fragments, aporetic word plays, etymologies, and fragmented language. Daesthetics illuminate language in the open, notes spaces of shut down, and offers alternate possibilities to subvert mastery in accelerating houses of language – that verge into the problem of judgment, closure, and totality.

---

[5] An unfilled space, a gap. A missing portion in a book or manuscript. Mid-17th century for pool or lake. Oxford Dictionary. https://www.lexico.com/definition/lacuna

[6] Imperfect texts; erasures; layered; erased historical texts

Daesthetics aims to work with uncertainty, to work into and on the lacunal unknowns, with finitude – *as elegies to what is missing in the archives*[7]. *Daesthetics, or death aesthetics is lacunal leaving, or what is missing in the text: the gaps, what is lost and the fragments of what remains.*

The Little Book of *Daesthetics* is not only a dictionary on the word daesthetics, but extended

---

[7] See *Archive Fever* by Jacques Derrida on how the archive is traced to the Greek word arkhé. The etymology is important because it means both "commandment" and "commencement," tying historically to authority, government, and law.

notes and musings on lacunal, fragmented, hidden, censored, and palimpsestic texts and works of art, offering a new way of seeing gaps in texts and what remains.

Daesthetics: a haunted house of language, is in remembrance of the liminal, archival gaps. Daesthetics, a thinking in the open, with the unknowing; is to suspend judgment - as there is something fragmented, lost, at times unknowable in the lacunal text.

Daesthetics is a contingent moment, it conveys the sense of the awe, as in the Sublime

of what is lost, gone, dead,
note also the puzzle aporias[8]
and indefinite alterities of the
missing text, the
paradox of what is
unknowable, yet known. A
daesthetics in finitude, is in
astonishment to
unfathomable time.
As time passes; an opening
into the question of a
poetics of language as a space
of fragmented undecidability
– which calls in to question
the problem of totalized
judgment, and the quandry of
forgetting finitude in what is
lost in the text. Daesthetics,
an aesthetics of the finite, is a

---

[8] Jacques Derrida, *Aporias.*

fragment of time, of the gap in the text.

The Little Book of Daesthetics is a composition of *fragments, lacunae, notes, entries, and poetical annotations.* Daesthetics questions the loss of the vitality of thinking because of the problem of injustice, censorship, and violence to alterity / to manuscripts. Daesthetics deals with the lacunae. The gap. The doubtful and uncertain on what is gone.

In What is Daesthetics? Or lacunal annotations, the idea of daesthetics opens thinking of possibility - the poetics inscribed in the aesthetics of the finite, of texts broken and cindered[9] in what remains barely visible. Death aesthetics, or daesthetics deals with Haunted texts, a hauntology of what is missing. Daesthetics, a thinking in finitude, is on the fragmentary text and a tribute to what remains, to the missing text, a sort of elegiac work remains.

The Little Book of Daesthetics opens with the question:
What is Daesthetics?
This book is a dictionary of finite--ontologies- -aporias,

---

[9] Allusion to Jacques Derrida's *Cinders*.

cryptologies; poetic
fragments, gaps, lacunae.

A Daesthetics of what is lost.
A lacunose, palimpsestic[10]
text.

- Lori Martindale

---

[10] Inscribed and reinscribed; partially erased; a metaphor for sociohistorical time and rewriting.

Lacunal Annotations

1 What is Daesthetics? 23

2 Daesthetics and Poetical Fragments 43

3 Daesthetics, Painting and Music 79

4 The Haunted House of Language 89

5 The Haunted Archive 145

6 Hypatia 155

7 On Painting: Artemisia Gentileschi 185

8 On a Blue
Daesthetics 201

9 Vanitas 229

10 Music, the Fleeting 275

11 Post-Scripts: Lacunal
Language 307

12 Lacunal Leavings,
Moths 329

"I declare,

That later on,

Even in an age unlike our own,

Someone will remember who we are."[11]

- Sappho

---

[11] Sappho, and Aaron Poochigian. *Stung with Love: Poems and Fragments*. London: Penguin Books, 2009. Print. P.87.

Welcome the music!
Let's hear the music of
suffering.[12]
Let's hear the lyre.

-Sappho Fragment 42
"Eros shakes my soul"

---

[12] Nietzsche: "…without music, life would be a mistake."

Chapter 1:

What is Daesthetics?

An aporia in open definition:

"To define is to limit."
— *Oscar Wilde*

But who is it that
is addressing
you?

- Jacques Derrida,
	Dissemination

> *"Writing is the
> passageway, the
> entrance, the exit,
> the dwelling place
> of the other in me"*
>
> *– Cixous*

What is Daesthetics?

/deTH/. The state of being dead.
/es THedik/ a philosophy of art.
Of the lacunae.

> 1. This question does not have one answer, for dictionary entries are broken open, puzzles: etymological aporias, wordplays.

These fractured
entries skip
across master
narratives,
traverse
uncertain
terrains, to resist
their snares and
trapped
enclosures.

*To cut into the finite is to cut
into poetic language in the
open.*

2. The question
here is on the
word daesthetics,
an aesthetics of

> the finite
> fragment.
> A monster.
> An aesthetics of
> finitude.
> An intersectional
> palimpsestic
> aesthetics of
> what has been
> lost and
> destroyed.

For what is a fragment but a broken piece of time? The fragment is the uncertainty of time. The Lacunae[13], the

---

[13] Latin: lăcūna (collateral form lŭcūna ; cf. Lachm. ad Lucr. vol. 2, p. 205; lăcūnā-tūra , App. Flor. 15, p. 351, 2 Hildebrand.
I.v. infra), ae, f. lacus, a ditch, pit, hole; esp. a place where water collects, a pool, pond.
I. Lit. (mostly poet.): lacuna, id est aquae collectio, a lacu derivatur, quam alii lamam, alii

lustrum dicunt, Paul. ex Fest. p. 117 Müll.: "vastae," Lucr. 6, 552: "vastae Orci," id. 1, 116; 6, 538: "cavae," Verg. G. 1, 117; 3, 365.—Poet.: "salsae," i. e. the sea, Lucr. 5, 794; 3, 1044; also, "Neptuniae," Auct. Her. 4, 10, 15: "caecas lustravit luce lacunas," Cic. Arat. 431.—

B. In gen., a hollow, cavity, opening, chasm, cleft: "cum supercilia cana, et sub ea lacunae, dicunt, eum equum habere annos sedecim," Varr. R. R. 2, 7, 3; 1, *29, 3*; cf.: "atque lacunarum fuerant vestigia cuique," Lucr. 5, 1261; Vitr. 7, 1, 4: "labrum superius sub ipsa medietate narium lacuna quadam levi, quasi valle, signavit deus," *Lact. Op. D. 10*: "genae teretes ac medio mento lacuna," *a dimple, App. Flor. p. 351* (Hildebr., lacunatura).—

II. Trop., *a gap, void, defect, want, loss* (rare but class.): "est, qui expleas duplicem istam lacunam," *to fill up the double void, Varr. R. R. 2, 1, 28*: "ut illam lacunam rei familiaris expleant," Cic. Verr. 2, 2, 55, § 138: "lacuna in auro," id. Att. 12, 6, 1: "illa labes et quasi lacuna famae," Gell. 1, 3, 23. Source: Etymology Dictionary. A Latin Dictionary. Founded on Andrews' edition of Freund's Latin dictionary. revised, enlarged, and in great

ellipses, the missing portions
of books and manuscripts.[14]
Daesthetics deals with the gap
in the text, the missing
illegible, weathering, lapse,
decay in manuscripts, the
long silences, missing
passages, the lacunae.[15]

---

part rewritten by. Charlton T. Lewis, Ph.D. and. Charles Short, LL.D. Oxford. Clarendon Press. 1879.

[14] Worm holes.

[15] 1. An extended silence in music. 2. A lapse in memory. 3. A lexical gap in language. Weathering, decay in manuscripts in which letters, words, sentences, and whole passages are gaps; missing; illegible.

Daesthetics[16]: palimpsestic[17]
texts, a text painted and
written, erased, fragmented,
inscribed, partly eaten by the
moths and worms of time.[18]

There is a scoring, slicing,
and tearing. The parchment is
erased and another
written, and again, scrambled
in intervals, where memory is
non-linear, and

---

[16] Daesthetics appeared in my essay "Ontologies of Leaving" in *On Leaving: Poetry, Daesthetics, Timelessness.*

[17] Metaphoric usage

[18] The association of writing and death with forgetfulness, with fly-by-night passing is a subject for literary texts rather than fertility which death brings, the becoming of leaving transforms writing to abundance in affirmation, opening a space for poesis to emerge in flight in ambivalence, which is a fruitfulness, a spell, charm, antidote.

fragmented in form. From the Latin palimpsestus, to clean parchment again for reuse, from the Greek palimpsēstos, again rubbed smooth, but palin again + also psēstos rubbed smooth, from psēn to scrape.

> 3. Daesthetics. An aesthetic of the finite fragment.
> b. lacunae; gaps in manuscripts, texts, inscriptions, paintings, or musical works.
> c. an interval in poetry.

d. papyrology.
E. textual criticism with finitude and or alterity in mind.
f. To postpone.
g. an alterity.
h. Unfinished works, often released posthumously.
i. To hide.
j. an undecidable.
k. a fragment.
L. bracketed ellipses […]
m. inscriptions; epitaphs.
N. finitude.
O. unknown.

- Daesthetics, a mixing and adding, a taking away, scraping; re-writing, on writing over. Plasticity[19]; an operation of writing, digging; heart transplant; uncovering; of craft; making and re-making art.

4. ~~The daesthetic text~~ is toward an aesthetics of scraping and rubbing smooth,

---

[19] Nietzsche

to uncover, to
see, if possible.
In the
margins of what
is forgotten, of
lacunal leaving;
a finitude in art
form but not
limited to;
aporias[20] of
leaving, in the
finite. Of
re-writing.
Daesthetics is
a hidden text,
inscribed,
fragmented,
erased,
re-written,

---

[20] See Jacques Derrida's *Aporias.*

a third text.
Removed.
A time-less-ness
as indeterminate
flux; an interval
in language,
aporetic
etymologies, lost
at sea.
A poetics of
departure; of
finitude; of
apertures in
language;
interplay;
fragments;
"Undecidabilities."[21]

---

[21] Derrida. Note: the word undecidable will be used in this text, always referring to Derrida on the undecidable. Derrida writes how undecidables "... situate perhaps better than others the places where discourses can no longer dominate, judge, decide: between the positive and the nega-

Fragments. What is in the
fragment can be remains,
wreckages, rubbish, "trash",
flotsam and jetsam, pieces,
bits, slivers, sections, portions,
parts, chips, scraps.

What is lost?
> 1. 4. In the British Library manuscript Cotton Vitellius A. xv, the Old English poem *Beowulf* contains the following lacuna:

---

tive, the good and the bad, the true and the false" (*Points*, p.86).

hyrde ich þæt
[... ...On]elan
cwen.
—*Fitt 1, line 62*
Editors attempt
to fill the gap
with "waes"
(was) or
because of the
alliteration with
Onela, Malone
explained (1929)
Yrse for the
unnamed
Queen.[22]
Of course this is
inconclusive.

---

[22] G. Jack, "Beowulf: A Student Edition. Oxford University Press. Oxford: 1994. Pp.31-32, footnote 62.

5. The eight-leaves-long *Great Lacuna* in the *Codex Regius*. *Völsunga saga (epic poetry)*.

6. In Codex Leicester, Acts 10:45 to 14:17 omitted.

7. The Epic of Gilgamesh / lacunae

8. Most of Tablet V of the Babylonian Creation Myth *Enûma Eliš*

has never been recovered

9. *The Latin poem Astronomica (Marcus Manilius A.D.30-40) lacuna in the 5th book.*

10. *El Cantar de mio Cid "the song of my Cid" the oldest preserved Castilian epic poem contains lacunae.*

11. Lacunae;
    a-daesthetics
    in Music: the
    caesura, a space
    of breath:

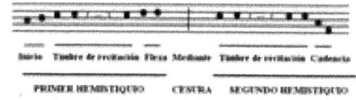

12. Sappho's
    fragments
    contain
    lacunae. Sappho
    is a nefelibata,
    a goddess muse
    of ancient Greek
    lyric poetry.

a. (death) aesthetics.
belles-lettres. Literature as art.
A study of the finitude in
literary arts.
3b. Daesthetics as
Nefelibata: (n). Lit. "Cloud
Walker", from ancient Greek
néphos (cloud) and latin
(nebula); bátēs, "walker";
as 1. Daydreamer.
2. One who does not follow
conventions.

Chapter 2

Daesthetics of Poetical Fragments[23]

Sappho

Toward a fragment-ology of the lacunose. Sappho offers a daesthetics, a poetics of the gap, the ellipses.

---

[23] This is a fragmented entry on poetical breaks, fragmented papyrus, in Sappho. For more on daesthetics, language, and poetry, see the book *On Leaving: Poetry, Daesthetics, Timelessness.*

αλλ' οθεν ιδιως καταδονται θηλυ
ν[.] γαρ τι καιτ' αλκιμον παιζέτε
οι δες υμιν παντες γε θεοι σε λογ. τη
.αττημοειεαι·
αλλα ται πτωντηνε δεκαι κενθωσι
πολλα..ες εσορ.ν..κ.υ.μ........
εδιξερον τιδες αλν ατοντα
μ.λχ[.]ισον·
κμμιες ιχρι νιατι.λεκει αλλα

παντα[.] τ' ιδωε συνεπι στοπ[.]υμεν
ευλιμη· εκμεςι αλν δητ[.]ω[.]
δι[.].
τωι κε βοαλντ λιβ[.]ε ιλευκοι υλπιω
δαμιοι ςεπτομωνετ' α..θωνιι δη
περ τγροπ ηνκημοιυ κατεςηεςοιται
και τυχοι αβοι·
αμμεοι κε αν κε.λ υιν δετ[.]..
λρι χοςει αμ του ταμ ιςγενη ται
α....αρτομηέ. ..τομμαι μεν
δι λλο θωμεν·
τιυς χι αν τιοου ομ.ν..λαοσ
κατηλεςωο[.]..... ειεκιν..
εεκομηαιτ.τ.. κα
ονεχιιροι
λοπε· αλειυτε...ε...
π[.]ωτ[.]ιν
στια..υ.αυυς·ν
ν ξερι

Image:

Fragment of a poem concerning her brother Charaxos and the second newly outed fragment is about love and Kypris (Aphrodite) poem. Fragment of Papyrus preserving parts of the two poems thought to be by Sappho. Published for the first time by Dirk Obblink in 2014; Public Domain. Dirk Obblink 'Two New Poems From Sappho', Zeitschrift für Papyrologie und Epigraphik 189 (2014) 32–49.

These fragments, full of lacunose, were lost to antiquity and discovered in 2013 in a mummy wrapping (shown to Oxford's Dr. Dirk Obblink in 2013 by an unnamed private collector in London). The scrap contains two poems. The first poem is missing the opening lines, though most of the text besides the opening lines survives. It seems the speaker is speaking to someone about her brother, a wine merchant who sails frequently for work. The younger brother is also mentioned, Larichus.

How much of the poem's lines have been lost is unknown? The poem is structured as an address to an unknown person on the speaker /poet's brother's safe return home at sea, and she will pray to Hera for Charaxus safe return. Because of seafaring and the absent loved one, the poem conjures up Homer's *Odyssey*.

The next poem "How could a person fail to ache / Queen Kypris, always for the one / she loves and, more than anything / wishes to come back again?" is on Queen Kypris /Aphrodite, where the speaker is conversing with Aphrodite "Please keep your eagerness in check, / since you called me here, in vain" (Lines 1-6). Then the fragment breaks down at the end of the line and becomes unclear. The papyrus ruins where the last four legible words reveal in between fragments of "to wound…desire…release…young…"

Poetic Opening

"I Seem a Ghost" – Sappho, *"phainetai moi"*

"My heart's grown heavy, my knees will not support me/… This state I oft bemoan; but what's to do? / Not to grow old, being human, there's no way"

- Sappho, Book IV.

Fragments. What is missing? Of course, ancient works are fragmented with time, the notable destroyer. The ellipses tell the reader there is something lost.

At what point is a manuscript ordered to death, executed,

however? What happens to its body, its voice, its remains? Poetry Foundation illustrates how Saint Gregory of Nazianzus, the bishop of Constantinople ordered Sappho's poems to be burned. Pope Gregory VII also ordered her works to be burned.[24]

The Library of Alexandria housed nine collections of her poetry before the library was burned down more than once.

---

[24] "Sappho" Poetry Foundation https://www.poetryfoundation.org/poets/sappho; *Poetry's Place in the History of Banned Books.*

Sappho's poems are labeled as fragments and numbers in 20th century translations. What remains today are the fragments of Sappho as a poet.

Sappho was in the archaic Greek world the famous Lyric poet from the Isle of Lesbos between 620 BCE to 550 BCE. Her lyric poetry together with the lyre brought her fame and now survives in lacunose fragments. Sappho is called the 10th Muse by Plato.

The poem "Ode to Aphrodite" is the only

complete poem which
remains, the rest are
fragments.

Such as the fragment which
survives on potsherd: "Leave
Crete and sweep to this blest
temple / Where apple
orchard's elegance / Is yours,
and smouldering altars, /
ample Frankincense"
survives only on a fragment
of broken pottery and is likely
a Kletic hymn. The spring
and autumn imagery fades
into fragility: "Here under
the boughs a bracing spring
/ Percolates, roses without
number / Umber the earth
and, rustling / The leaves drip

slumber" (lines 5-9). The leaves of "drip slumber" evoke a deep, special sleep induced in the landscape.

/deTH/. The state of being dead.
/es THedik/ a philosophy of art.
Ancient vases, statues, and frescos of her image date back to BCE, such as this one by the famous vase painter who is called the Brygos Painter, from 470 B.C.

Daesthetics as Poems in Conversation:

The daesthetics (/deTH/. The state of being dead. /es THedik/ a philosophy of art).
of fragmentary notations – metaphoric Palimpsestic[25] texts in translation.

Fragment 31 "That man seems to me to be equal to the gods / who is sitting opposite you" survives only because Longinus (writing in Greek during the Roman Empire) included the fragment in his *On the Sublime* *circa 1st*

---

[25] Sociohistorical time as imperfect; erasure; imperfect and partly visible texts; layered inscribed coffin texts; mummy wrappings.

century C.E.), on aesthetics and literary loftiness. Longinus raises the question "Are you not astonished?" in his essay on the sublime as "the most extreme and intense expression of emotion" which is also lovesickness.

On the Sublime was translated into English by John Hall 1652, and Nicolas Boileau-Despréaux's French translation of Longinus (1674) also introduced readers to Sappho's Fragment 31.

Sappho was the first to call love bittersweet (poem 130).

This lovesickness can cause uncertainty, sleeplessness.

In Fragment 31, Eros the trickster appears. The transient nature of Eros appears in the somatic imagery of erotic desire as a flame, a fever, and melting. The symptoms of fever caused by the lovesickness, the erotic is described in Fragment 31, as translated by Roman poet Catullus to contemporary Canadian poet and translator of ancient Greek, Anne Carson. Carson calls "the blind point in Eros is a paradox of time as well as in space" (Eros the Bittersweet,

111). Carson discusses how the ancient Greek poets imagine desire as heat and the image of Eros as a "melter." Eros, with wings, is of the air. Eros is liminal, desire in-between the sublime and death. Carson describes Eros as "wedged between two senses" with those wings, hovering between with "heart and chest on wings." The desire is a reaching for the unknown.

In *Eros the Bittersweet*, Carson discusses how Eros eludes as a blind point and vanishes in the Phaedrus between Phaedrus and Sokrates: "If you reach into the Phaedrus to get ahold of Eros, you will

be eluded, necessarily" (167).
Eros takes flight each time.
Time is a poetic metaphor, a
fleeting death.

"A thinking mind is not swallowed up by what it comes to know"

-Anne Carson

To begin with a translation of
Fragment 31 by John Hall,
a translation of Longinus, in
the attempt to bring Sappho's
work into a 1652
conversation - in the tradition
of the lyric. The poem's
speaker is near death,
trembling with Eros.

Here is the second half of
"*phainetai moi*", translated by
John Hall (1652):

I'm speechless, feavrish, fires
    assail
My fainting flesh, my sight
doth
    fail
Whilst to my restless mind
my
    ears
Still hum new fears.

Cold sweats and tremblings so
    invade
That like a wither'd flower I
fade
So that my life being almost
lost,
    I seem a Ghost.

I seem a Ghost.

In his influential work, "On Sublimity," Longinus[26] praises Sappho's choice of detail and presentation of conflicting emotions as the source of sublimity in her work. Longinus particularly refers to poem 31 and states, "We see in her not a single emotion, but a complex of emotions. Lovers experience all of this; Sappho's excellence, as I have said, lies in her adoption and combination of the most striking details" ("On Sublimity," 141). In Fragment, Poem 31, for

---

[26] Longinus. "On Sublimity."

instance, the speaker captures the seemingly incongruous elements of hot and cold feeling in the body "fire is racing under the skin...and cold sweat holds me" (lines 10-13). This complex physical feeling corresponds to the varying emotions that rage within the speaker, from wings lifting the heart to the wounding feeling of death.

As Longinus indicates, not only does this capturing of the proper conflicting details correspond to the experiences of lovers, but it elevates the poem to the level of sublime expression that leads to the passion of wonder. The experience of being dead, or almost, (as Anne Carson's translation indicates), reflects an experience of almost, not quite, of the uncertain stumbling sensation of being gripped by the liminality of Eros and the unimaginable finitude.

Anne Carson's fragment
translation in *If Not, Winter*,
fragment 31:

no speaking
    is left in me
no: tongue breaks and thin
fire is racing under skin
and in eyes no sight and
drumming
    fills ears

and cold sweat holds me and
shaking
grips me all, greener than
grass
I am and dead—or almost
    I seem to me.

I am and dead – or almost

- Sappho

To One who Loved
not Poetry[27]

- Sappho

---

[27] This English translation by Edwin Arnold is from Greek Poets in English verse, ed. William Hyde Appleton. Cambridge: Riverside Press, 1893.

THOU liest dead, and there will be no memory left behind

Of thee or thine in all the earth, for never didst thou bind

The roses of Pierian streams upon thy brow; thy doom

Is now to flit with unknown ghosts in cold and nameless gloom

The nameless gloom, unknown ghosts, "thou liest dead" offers a glimpse into the uncertainty of becoming unknown if one "loves not poetry."

It is as if poetry keeps the listener alive, a contingent spell.

Sappho's poems are made of what is called "Sapphic stanzas." Sapphic stanzas are four-line stanzas. The first 3 lines are Hendecasyllablic (meaning there are 11 syllables per line, this comes from the Greek word for 11). This is an ancient form of poetry accredited to Sappho, and she wrote them to be accompanied by the "lyre" instrument (which is Greek where the word "lyric" is derived). The heart of the line is the choriamb (-uu-).

Here is an example of the 11-syllable line:

x x - u u - u - u - -

(where x x is either - u or - - or u -)

Note the Hendecasyllable lines:

"Glittering-Minded deathless Aphrodite,"
xx -uu- u-u

Fragment 94:

> I just really want to die.
> She, crying many tears, left me
> And said to me:
> "Oh, how terribly we have suffered, we two,
> Sappho, really I don't want to go away."
> And I said to her this:
> Go and be happy, remembering me,
> For you know how we cared for you.

And if you don't I
want to remind you
.............and the
lovely things we felt
with many wreathes
of violets
and ro(ses and cro)
cuses
and.............. and
you sat next to me
and threw around
your delicate neck
garlands fashioned
of many woven
flowers
and with
much...............
costly myrrh
.............and you

> anointed yourself
> with royal.....
> and on soft
> couches.......(your)
> tender.......
> fulfilled your
> longing.........[28]

Sappho's fragment 94 (damaged; the Papyrus is full of lacunae and fragmented– what is lost?).

The speaker begins with saying how she simply wants to die (1). Many readers see this poem as sorrow, though

---

[28] Translation William Harris, Middlebury College, Classics.

the following lines do not simply despair in longing, but also cherish the memories of her beloved, which creates a rich meditation on love. She describes a lover, her as weeping with sorrow to miss Sappho in the future, shifting back to memory of her loss. The speaker insists on recalling "the beautiful times we had" (11) and in following her memory describes indulgent images of "many woven garlands / made of flowers / around your soft throat." The speaker yearns for what has passed; reflects calmly and poetically on the departed lover.

Poetical Fragments

Οἶον τὸ γλυκύμαλον
ἐρεύθεται ἄκρῳ ἐπ' ὄσδῳ,
ἄκρον ἐπ'ἀκροτάτῳ,
λελάθοντο δὲ μαλοδρόπηες·
οὐ μὰν ἐκλελάθοντ', ἀλλ'
οὐκ ἐδύναντ' ἐπίκεσθαι.

From Sappho, Fragment
105a[29]

---

[29] Source: Sappho Fragment 105a. *Poetry* translated by Anita George, 1994.

You: an Achilles' apple

Blushing sweet on a high branch

At the tip of the tallest tree.

You escaped those who would pluck your fruit.

Not that they didn't try. No,

They could not forget you

Poised beyond their reach.

130

---

[30] *Sappho Kissing Her Lyre.* Jules-**Élie** Delaunay. Public Domain.

The Little Book of *Daesthetics* | 77

Chapter 3:

A Daesthetics, Painting and Music

The Jules-Élie Delaunay (1828-1891) painting of Sappho, kissing her lyre, is one where the lyre itself replaces the figure of the subject. Her lyre is the erotic subject of poetics and music. The lyre itself becomes an organ, an instrument of the poetic erotic outside of the patriarchal world; the lyre replaces the phallus. A song of poetry reciprocal of the utterance that always already

flies outside of a closed structure. A doubling of two forces which join to achieve an unheard economy: in a dislocated time, a contemporaneous exchange of the unknowable other which plunges into a depth of language, of remembering the dead through song…
An opening of the time of two: poetics and music.

The lyre is a giant ear and organ of poetry, of the feminine. A medusa.[31]
A daesthetics of music; a giant ear in the open.

Painting as Kinesthetics.

---

[31] See Cixous, "The Laugh of the Medusa."

Image:

The painting is a response to the death of the sparrow, as death to life.
Where is the poem to the painting? The painting to the music of the palimpsest text? A text inscribed and re-inscribed such that the text is imperfectly erased, only partly visible. Notes of the lacunae. Historical time is only partly visible, an imperfect erasure, the past always visible in the present.

Is the poem, over the edge?
In excess? An overflow?

In "Parergon," the ancient Greek supplement, an extra or embellishment, Derrida asks what is not of a work of art? Does it have an end and a beginning? What is a frame? Is ornament of a work of art, or outside of it?

The fragmentary, palimpsestic[32] poem, like the painting, is outside the frame, a daesthetic overflow, an edge of certainty that one will disappear. The poem is outside of time. The painting

---

[32] Layered, scraped, a text beneath a text

a response to time. Both
lacunal to time and present.

... Ἔλθε, Κύπρι,
Χπρυσίασιν ἐν κυλίκεσσιν
ἄβραισ
συμμεμιγμένον θαλίαισι
νέκταρ
  οἰνοχόεισα.

Come, goddess of Cyprus,
and in golden cups serve
nectar delicately mixed with
delights.

Come hither foam-born
Cyprian goddess, come,
And in golden goblets pour
richest nectar
All mixed in most ethereal
perfection,
    Thus to delight us.

The fragment is part of an invocation to Aphrodite.[33]

Sappho Fragment 42
"Eros shakes my soul"

---

[33] Quoted by Athenaeus, who wrote in the first half of the third century C.E.

Chapter 4:

The Haunted House of Language

1. ... (Ellipses; caesura)

2. Daesthetics: a haunted house of language. Like Derrida's hinge[34] mechanisms, a differance, "to leave" hinges on the infinite exits into alternate spacings of language as passing aperture. Leaving, not reduced to one stable meaning,

---

[34] The Derridean hinge of language; one of discontinuity through language and rupture in writing.

never present, in the threshold, only traces of traces, a windswept page. Daesthetics is in the fragmented scraps of papyrus; Book of the Dead: coffin texts.

3. The "time-less aesthetics of death" or "daesthetics"[35] is a meditation on the aporetic elegiacs of leaving, in the etymology of the word "to leave," as written time, which illustrates time-less-ness (timeless

---

[35] On emphasis of word daesthetics: on and of death, toward an aesthetics of leaving and writing, of "death."

as not frozen, fixed, or determinate, though of flux; contemporaneous, moving, indeterminate) as an almost absent palimpsestic[36] bewilderment. Poetic doubt. Negative capability.[37] The palimpsestic[38] text is the fragmented, non-linear memory in leaving; the wreckage. Daesthetics resists containment, totalized judgments in the recognition of finitude.

---

[36] erasure
[37] Of what John Keats calls "negative capability." The poet's ability to exist in uncertainty and curiosity, doubt, mystery.
[38] Sociohistorical erasure

4. The terror, horror, monstrosity, yet familiarity, remembrance, affinity, to leaving is never the same, never identical to itself.
To leave is a motion in finitude, paradoxically continuous illusion of flickering memory, exceeding reason to undecidablility, as in *sublime time.*[39] *Leaving is the poet.* To leave ~~changes~~, *incommensurable.*

---

[39] Allusion to the Romantic Sublime; horrors of being in the world; Kantian Sublime; Edmund Burke's aspects of "the sublime." I coined "sublime time" as a horror in magnitude of the finite.

5. There is a haunting in the undecidable.[40] Finitude here is a place of unjudging, of undecidable wonder, a space of mysterious paradox.

6. In Derrida's *The Gift of Death*, the self's passage into death, into the individuality is irreproducibility. In *Demeure*, when Derrida reads Blanchot's *The Instant of My Death*, (Blanchot's third

---

[40] Where does the poet wander to, in this gift of death? "For in that sleep of death what dreams may come, / When we have shuffled off this mortal coil, / must give us pause - " (*Hamlet*).

person narrative of his near-death execution through the agency of the Russian Nazi firing squad in 1944), he concludes "when one is dead, it does not happen twice, there are not two deaths even if two die" (67). Blanchot's memory is chronicled in *The Instant of My Death*, as it actually took place, and the writing places the experience into a third person young man.

7. Daesthetics: A person's death is a definition

of life and of time, a timing that cannot be repeated.

7a. Derrida considers Blanchot's life after the unexperienced experience of assassination as a "moratorium of an encounter of the death outside of him with the death that is already dying in him" and upholds the moment of the death of that instant, despite the undying (Demeure, 95). The material instance of mortality which Derrida reads in Blanchot's text is the disappearance of a manuscript in his house at the time of the execution, which Derrida calls "a mortal text", a great loss -"a death without a survivance" (100). The text is akin to the corpse. A body of work, of life. The act of reading the text is an act of survivance. Mourning by reading is a way to the authors memory.

8. Derrida points out the paradox of Death itself as a gift, but not a present, without "fact of being seen" (29).

9. Mourning is duplicated in Derrida's work through the experience of looking at photographs.

10. Derrida explores how mourning breaks down or stammers. In other words, there is a daesthetic ... breakdown or fracturing of language in mourning.

11. In his remembering
    of Jan Patočka, Derrida
    memorializes his friend.

Question:

What is Daesthetics?

Answer:

To Be is to Be haunted by manuscripts. Or the mysterious lacunae.

12. To Be Haunted is the Haunted House of Language, a cryptographic dismantling and remembering - those who have been murdered, and or forgotten. Hearing the phantoms in the haunted house of language.

13. Daesthetics: the dirge.

a. In Avital Ronell's text *Complaint, Grievance Among Friends*, Ronell explores the complaint's relationship to grievance and to mourning. What is not there invites the reader to view the ghostly, the unseen, the undecidable, the non-present, and to defy the undefinable. This invites lamentation, the dirge, the poet.

13.b. A ghost story Sound effects: There is a storm outside the house of language, a window, an aperture, open. Where does the poet wander to, in this "gift of death"[41]?

---

[41] Allusion to Shakespeare; Derrida's *The Gift of Death*

Aside: "Never Shall I depart from Sorrow
And tears and lamentation"

(Sophocles *Electra*, 231-232).

Avital Ronell's text *Stupidity*, a key text on the importance of thinking, on the significance of unknowability and suspension of judgment. The Undecidable.

To be uncertain before "the other" is thinking, a bow before the other (66). An opening in friendship. There is also a to be stupid before the finite. In thinking. There is an unknowability; an undecidability of finitude. Stupidity is the undecidable; a daesthetic text of thinking in mourning, a doubling of the uncertain daesthetic trope.

An indecision.
Phantoms between writing
and voices of the texts.

"The poet - or more exactly,
the poem - is subordinated to
the passage of time."

- Avital Ronell,
Stupidity

Il y a là cendre (Derrida).

Stupidity is a Nietzschean tight rope walk in daesthetics: "Does not the philosophical life always accept its fate as a mindful relation to death, whether imposed and inscribed (Socrates) or repelled and inscribed (Kant, Nietzsche)?" (Stupidity, 299). Is death in the word, infinite finite vouloir-dire, in the fragility of the reply, in the unstable indeterminant limit (Derrida; Ronell).

Ronell writes in Nietzschean courage on the existential leap of the poet:

"If the poet needs to be coaxed in the direction of the living and is shown to be tempted by temporality to the extent that it ensures passage and passing, this is in part due to the fact that the inaugural recession marked by the poem as it exhorts, invites, pushes toward the living, begins in nonlife. This extreme passivity, the near stupor characteristic of the poetic disposition, situates itself dangerously close to the side of depletion and even death, which is why the poet has to be roused and jump-started with deceptive promise: 'Then just wander forth defenseless / Through life and have no care!'" ("The Poet's Courage" 1:21; *Stupidity*, 9).

14. The pluck of the poet marks the fragility of language, but also the risk of death, of not knowing where the poet is traversing, into the darkness.

For Cixous, *l'ecriture feminine* is within poetic language.

The lacunae, a gap, an opening into time.
Daesthetics is an opening, a writing of the lacunae.
A fabric of contingency.

15. Derrida, in *Cinders*
thinks with mourning,
on "the urn of language"
and fragility: "But the
urn of language is so
fragile. It crumbles and
immediately you blow
into the dust of words
that are the cinder itself.
And if you entrust it to
paper, it is all the better
to enflame you with, my
dear; you will eat
yourself up with
immediately" (35).
The tomb and work of
mourning, a paper time;
a palimpsestic[42] gap,
flame.

---

[42] Erased; reinscribed; imperfectly erased and partly visible texts; metaphor for sociohistorical time

How many manuscripts, canvases enflamed and spectral? Derrida explains Cinders are "the better paradigm for what I call the trace-something that erases itself totally, radically, while presenting itself" (Derrida, Cinders). The erasure of itself, the specter appearance.

"In this sentence I see the tomb of a tomb…"

- Derrida,
Feu la cendre

Derrida's first words on *Of Spirit: Heidegger and the Question*: "I shall speak of a ghost, of flame, and of ashes."

Daesthetic Spectrality haunts the undecidable page.
As Samuel Coleridge explains: "suspend disbelief."

15a. Indeed, palimpsest texts are spectral texts, a

daesthetic trope in haunting, the double structure already at work in the text. What was mutilated in a ~~text~~, destroyed, scraped out or burned?

15b. Mourning destroyed texts.

16. Daesthetics as Art; suspension of judgment.
B. An alterity.
c. On the Question as a possibility; an aporia; a way out: To question

the backlash against the
Humanities - theory, art,
and thinking – a
totalitarian judgment
against art, against
thinking; a shut-down
or lock-down, a
straitjacket to thinking.
An attempted silence,
attempted murder of art.
Closure is a
judgment; thinking
shuts down. Passing
judgment, intolerance
is a closure, a refusal or
finality, a metaphysical
totalization
conceptualization,

which does not allow for possibility, for alterity. Thinking with the question offers a way out. There is continuous movement, a freeplay[43]

---

[43] Derrida explains in his important essay "Structure, Sign, and Play in the Discourse of the Human Sciences": "Besides the tension of freeplay with history, there is also the tension of freeplay with presence. Freeplay is the disruption of presence. The presence of an element is always a signifying and substitutive reference inscribed in a system of differences and the movement of a chain. Freeplay is always an interplay of absence and presence, but if it is to be radically conceived, freeplay must be conceived of before the alternative of presence and absence; being must be conceived of as presence or absence beginning with the possibility of freeplay and not the other way around" (294).

(Derrida) which "opens up" and "makes possible" without the confines of a total structure in the question. The question can be an act of resistance. To be (a nod to Karl Popper) intolerant of intolerance as an opening to ethics; a suspension of judgement.

17. To remember leaving is ineffable; it is to put finitude in thought. A daesthetics of *Leaving* illuminates

ethical possibilities to subvert mastery in accelerating houses of language of totalized judgments, with finitude in the ear, to be open in unknowing. Through a slow poetics of the intervals – opens a haunting deep time in remembrance, a deceleration media of leaving in the thresholds. "To leave" hinges on the infinite exits into alternate spacing of language as timelessly-as-moving aperture, a passing by. Time-less-ness has traditionally been equated with the classic eternal[44] stationary, unmoving, illusory binary as "permanent," likened with a metaphysically fixed dimension of "The Word/Reason," equated with "truth" and "all knowing." To throw this into question is to leave through the gap, aporias.

---

[44] Late 14c., from Old French eternel or directly from Late Latin aeternalis, from Latin aeternus "of an age, lasting, enduring, permanent, endless," contraction of aeviternus "of great age," from aevum "age" (*Chambers Etymology*).

18. Thresholds of haunted time.

19. A passing, what is hidden, what haunts being. A blurring of more than two. A third space, opening to another.
   a. Daesthetics: a leaving.

   "Everything ends with flowers."
   　　　　　　- Cixous

   The poet
   is double in time and
   space – the poet goes

into the world of the dead, feasts with the dead, and returns, speaking from the leaves. To quote Rilke: "You have to sit down and eat / with the dead, sharing their poppies, / if you want enough memory to keep / the most delicate note…"[45]

20. The book (written text, the novel, the epic, for instance) in its written form, the reader can continue to read the words of the dead; the

---

[45] Rilke, Sonnet 9 to Orpheus.

reader can communicate with the dead through the written text. The reader can ask a question, and the answer, possibly a riddle, in the enigmatic written text of the endless enigma. The ineffable. Infinity is finitude; with the dead, one is in the other (death and fecundity, life). What is a book?

21.a. Leave: to depart. To bid farewell.[46] The contemporaneous motion of leaving is akin to death and time in

---

[46] O.E.D. pp.776.

textum,[47] in a freeplay of finitude (as a limited space, never stagnant, meaning always slips away); a poison and antidote,[48] the affirmation: no space permanent; timeless as fixed: there is flux, moving, leaving, changing, and, to invoke a Derridean aporia: différance as time (defer, differ); in perishing.[49]

22. Unfathomable time, memory, a memento

---

[47] The textum web of language; the web of life and of the dead; a double.

[48] The pharmakon, see Derrida's "Plato's Pharmacy."

[49] See Derrida's text *Aporias.*

mori,[50] in variation continuous, "passing from one state to another."

23. Even in leaving. passing, Derrida explains "freeplay is the disruption of presence" – there is finitude disrupting, there is constant flux and motion, freeplay in language as a fading away in time, an infinite play through the doorways of the haunted

---

[50] Memento mori: *Latin.* "Remember that you will die."

house of language,
moving through, a
passing.
Leaving is an
etymology: a
communicative model
of leaving one to
another word in radical
departures, freeplay. The
signifier leaves the sign
into a radical departure
from tradition, as can
be seen in the
deconstruction of the
word "leave" in all of its
variation.[51] (To go,
to give, to die, to exit,

---

[51] Variations of the word "leave" throughout this text; see also chapter two and subsequent chapters.

to depart, to grow, to postpone, pages in a book, to postpone, to defer…etc). What is left behind?

24. *An allusion from Leaving, Leave*, Entry 14: "a. leave behind. (Also, to leave behind one).
(a) To neglect, leave undone (obs).
(b) not to take with one at one's departure, to go away without.
(c) to have remaining after departure or

removal, as a trace[52] or consequence.
(d) to outstrip" (O.E.D., 778).

25. Daesthetics, a decentering of the interval between time and space in language, a poetics of finitude[53] which resists closure in an unnamable process of thinking the question. The spacing interval is a spacing for a possibility of deep time as postponement, an

---

[52] Derrida on trace.
[53] See Derrida/John Caputo *Deconstruction in a Nutshell* "That opening breaks the spell of present closure, allowing the present to be haunted by ghosts" (154).

aperture of leaving, and of deferral.[54] It is this space between language, a space of infinite relation, which finds an interval in variantology of undecidability in time, a leaving in continual relativity…

---

[54] Derrida on deferral. Différance as time *ad infinitum* (defer, postpone; to be unlike, unidentical); to differ, to defer. "différence". *Différance (to* différer means to defer and to differ. Words can never be fully what they mean, they appeal to additional words. Meaning is postponed, endlessly. Différance is in continual flux. In addition, on the trace: in *Speech and Phenomena*, Derrida discusses how the "now" is always finding middle; compromised by a trace (62).

26. death + aesthetics=
daesthetics/ Finitude.

27. Daesthetics: What is left behind?
Leave I: "to have a remainder; to cause to allow to remain."
Leave 2a: "To transmit at one's death."
3a. "To be left. To remain. To abstain from taking, removing." "To leave the earth. To die. To leave the field. Retreat."
4. To neglect or perform. To leave undone.

b. to allow to stand over, to postpone.
c. "To leave to be desired, to wish."
II. To depart from, go away, relinquish.
7a. To deviate from.[55]

28. To leave as remainder, passing, a memory. One can't control how much to remember; memorialize. From mid-13th c. To remember is a call to recollection, awareness, consciousness. From French memorie "mind,

---

[55] Oxford English Dictionary. pp.777.

memory, remembrance, memorial, record" and Latin "mind, remembrance, faculty of remembering." The memory of awareness, in Greek, merimna or "caring" and mermeros "causing anxiety, mischievous, baneful" Serbo-Croatian mariti "to care for" and Welsh marth "sadness, anxiety", Old English gemimor "known" and "murnan" or mourn and remember sorrowfully. Dutch *mijmeren "to ponder" the giant.*

29. *The Giant: Old Norse Mimir* "a giant who guards the well of wisdom."

30. To remember is to memorialize, an echoic memory. Does one know when one has been forgotten?

30. The undecidable (spectral figures, time, the infinite), of finitude thus conjecture itself in language toward an experience of the formless, of leaving, in a radical un-signification of alterity. Leaving implies

an ontological labyrinthine continuation, an opening not of horizon, a motion between, moving through, passing by, aporia, "to leave behind," death and remains of memory, elegiac time, a waiting within movement. The elegiac, an aperture, an ethics for remembrance, which reflects lamentation and possibility for the affirmation of alterity and the (in)finite in a spacing of unfathomable time.

32. Daesthetics:
    Aesthetics of the finite.

    Time-less-ness, a
    reminder of the subject
    death, to leave, to have
    less time, yet
    paradoxically, to remain
    (in the fecundity of
    writing). There is
    Mnemosyne.
    Memory haunts the
    subject, which decenters
    a line between the living
    and the dead.
    What is forgotten?
    Does one know when
    one is in the realm of
    memory?
    Of recalling?

Can one control or know when one is remembered, or when one is forgetting? There is an unknowing in the possibility of memory. What is forgetting, which comes and goes? Memory is also a forgetting. The palimpsestic text always has holes in it, there are forgotten and scraped out texts, inscribed and re-inscribed until the previous text is only partly visible – sociohistorical time is an imperfect erasure.

Does one know what one forgets? The memory of forgetting is an impossibility of certainty of what one knows. One is always missing out and seeing what others cannot see, there is an unknowability in referentiality, and always already leaves behind a memory of what another does not know. This brings the text back to the figure of the fool. The question is a risk taking, a being suspended in unreliable narratives, of saying

what one knows might
get them axed. The
fool jumps through the
opening of the text.

33. To Haunt: to Be is to
    Be haunted.

    To Be is to Be haunted.
    Audre Lorde wrote and
    spoke about how "The
    Master's tools will never
    Dismantle the Master's
    House." Lorde's
    brilliant essay is about
    how the master's house
    is a language of
    patriarchal, racist, sexist,
    homophobic capital

colonialism, - which needs to be dismantled, but not with the same silencing, oppressive tools or the problem of systemic oppression remains. Lorde says to reach down inside to root the fear of difference, like racism, sexism, and homophobia, out. Audre Lorde is a genius deconstructionist.

"Poetry is not a luxury"

-Audre Lorde

Hauntology. The House
is … Haunted.
The house of language is
Haunted.
A need for dismantling.

A return from the past.
The house needs to be
dismantled, opened, the
aperture …

The house of language is
haunted by ghosts.
To leave is a break in
narrative through a

threshold, a door, a way
out through language
out of the house. To
wake after sleep.

The need to collaborate
is still yet waiting in the
world. The need to do
the work in the
systemic structure is
still in waiting. Always
already haunted by the
house.

"It is in the knowledge of
the genuine conditions of
our lives that we must draw
our strength to live and our
reasons for acting"

-Simone de Beauvoir

Double it up.
Opening; Language:
An aperture in
ontologies. The
"time-less aesthetics of
death" or "daesthetics"[56]
is a meditation on the
aporetic elegiacs of
leaving the house, in the
etymology of the word
"to leave," as written
time, which illustrates
language as not frozen,
fixed, closed, or
determinate, but of
flux; contemporaneous,
moving, indeterminate),
open as an almost absent

---

[56] …emphasis of word daesthetics: on dasein (crossed out), as death, toward an aesthetics of the finite, leaving and writing, in the open, of finitude, passing, to be in "death."

bewilderment.[57]
The terror, horror, monstrosity, yet familiarity, remembrance, affinity, leaving is never the same, never identical to itself. To leave is a motion in finitude, paradoxically continuous in an illusion of flickering memory, exceeding reason to undecidablility, as in *sublime time.*[58]

---

[57] Of what John Keats calls "negative capability." The poet's ability to exist in uncertainty and curiosity, mystery.

[58] Allusions to the Romantic Sublime "horrors of being in the world," such as the Kantian Sublime in *Observations on the Feeling of the Beautiful and Sublime,* and Edmund Burke's book *A Philo-*

> *Leaving is the poet.* To leave changes, *incommensurable.*

33 cont. A-Daesthetics of Leaving illuminates ethical possibilities to subvert mastery in accelerating houses of language of totalized judgments, with finitude in the breath of life, to be open in unknowing. Death is the great unknown, the deep mystery, the undecidable. Through

---

sophical Enquiry…
I coined "sublime time" as horror in magnitude of time and gaps of time, a lacunal myopia.

a slow poetics of the intervals – opens a haunting deep time in remembrance, a deceleration media of leaving in the thresholds. "To leave" hinges on the infinite exits into alternate spacing of language as cinematic, timelessly-as-moving aperture. Time-less-ness has traditionally been equated with the classic eternal,[59] stationary,

---

[59] Late 14c., from Old French eternel or directly from Late Latin aeternalis, from Latin aeternus "of an age, lasting, enduring, permanent, endless," contraction of aeviternus "of great age," from aevum "age" (*Chambers Etymology*).

unmoving, "permanent," likened with a metaphysically fixed dimension of "The Word/Reason," equated with "truth" and "all knowing." The master's house is at a near point of collapse.

Chapter 5

The Haunted Archive

34a. Daesthetics: remembering and reading texts that have been black-listed and destroyed due to totalitarianism fascism.[60]

---

[60] The Nazi Book Burnings where books were burned that were deemed subversive and represented ideologies opposed to Nazism, they were burned. Books destroyed in the 1933 book burnings were murdered by fascism. Books by left, democratic, and Jewish literature, were destroyed. Resistance texts, Queer and trans inclusive texts were also destroyed. The Haunted Archives. The black-lists ranged from artists and authors such as Bebel, Bergengruen, Brod, Brecht, Einsten, Freud, the Mann Brothers, Schüler, to Marx and Kafka.

It is locating and finding, building an archive of murdered texts from the ashes. These texts are important to history and humanity as a collective. What gets added to the archive? What doesn't? In *Archive Fever* by Derrida, he discusses how the archive is traced to the Greek word arkhé. The etymology is important because it means both "commandment" and "commencement," tying historically to authority, government, and law.

34b. Anti-fascist leaflets. The importance of. Remembering activists like Sophia Scholl 1921-1943. German student and anti-Nazi resistance activist. Part of the White Rose Resistance group.[61] A non-violent intellectual resistance group led by Hans and Sophie Scholl, also Christoph Probst, Alexander Schmorell, Willi Graf, and professor of Musicology and Philosophy Kurt

---

[61] The White Rose Resistance group authored six leaflets, about 15,000 copies were circulated. They denounced Nazi crimes and oppression.

Huber, amongst other students and supporters. They had a non-violence resistance campaign that called for active opposition to the Nazi regime. Hans and Sophie Scholl, also Christoph Probst were arrested and executed by guillotine February 22, 1943. During trial defendants were not given the opportunity to speak during the Nazi Court, and many were sentenced to death or imprisonment. But even Sophie Scholl's last words stir the listener into direct action for freedom from tyranny: "Such a fine, sunny day, and I have to go…What does my death matter, if through us, thousands of people are awakened and stirred to action?"[62]

34c. Remembering archives. Magnus Hirschfeld. A queering of space and language. Eve Sedgewick wrote *The Epistemology of the Closet*.[63]

---

[62] Simkin, John (January 2016). "Sophie Scholl" Spartacus Educational. Retrieved September 8, 2020.

[63] Magnus Hirschfeld, Institute of Sexual Sciences, Berlin. Hirschfeld coined the term sexuelle Zwischenstufen or "sexual intermediaries" to explain infinite sexual desires and sexual bodies.

Daesthetics is also an in-between space, a gap in history. Lacunae. A liminality. What gets "lost" from the archives? In the case of Queer Feelings by Sarah Ahmed, the experience of encountering the problem of homophobia, racism, and sexism[64] as a violence, of a taking from the other. Ahmed discusses how homophobia and racism is the effect of

---

[64] Ahmed says they owe a lot to Audre Lorde in their book *Living a Feminist Life.*

someone trying "to steal the feeling of joy" (Ahmed; Žižek). Magnus Hirschfeld, Institute of Sexual Sciences, Berlin: the institute was raided, books were burned.[65] Michel Foucault famously said, in his Archaeology of Knowledge, how "The

---

[65] To critique closure and totalitarian fascist thinking as dangerous to knowledge, alterity, life, and community.
ii. Books / lacunae / palimpsestic hidden texts destroyed. Texts banned, burned. Not just of lost due to moths, worms, and time but murdered texts
In this case of the Institute of Sexual Sciences, this was also an attempt to eradicate trans history, queer (as a critique of all things oppressively normal, especially conventional ideas about sex) archives, culture, and history.

archive is the first law of what can be said, the system which governs the appearance of statements as unique events" (1972:129). The archive is a regulation of classical knowledge during the Renaissance, and to classical and modern knowledge for Foucault, where Derrida returns to Greek antiquity to study the arkheion, those who commanded the archive, such as magistrates who command the archive as a privileged space.

What is remembered, historically, in privileged and marginalized spaces?[66]

35. Rebellion.[67] Lacunal aperture. Fast Forward. Stonewall Riots. The Riot at Compton Cafeteria, and more. Aperture.

36. As listening.

37. Daesthetics as a house rebellion. An opening into the narrative.

---

[66] The past visible in the present
[67] Palimpsestic as a metaphor for social change. The past is visible in the present. To open the text.

A demand to be heard.
To be remembered as a
house.

38. xx. Daesthetics,
definition xx. a haunted
house; a haunted
metamorphosis of
language, art and life; a
bringing forth, a change,
an unearthing,
sometimes showing itself
or surprising; to notice.
Of Alterity. To change.

39. "Life is Metamorphosis"

   -Anne Dufourmantelle

Chapter 6:

Hypatia

40. Daesthetic Hypatia[68]

---

[68] Hypatia is known to have edited Book III of Ptolemy's Almagest. By Fastfission - From Edward Grant, "Celestial Orbs in the Latin Middle Ages", Isis, Vol. 78, No. 2. (Jun., 1987), pp. 152-173. See also: F. A. C. Mantello and A. G. Rigg, "Medieval Latin: An Introduction and Bibliographical Guide", The Catholic University of America Press, p. 365 (on-line text here)., Public Domain, https://commons.wikimedia.org/w/index.php?curid=317560

Schema huius præmissæ diuisionis Sphærarum.

41. Hypatia, 355-415 C.E.
   A martyr for philosophy.

"Where there is power, there is resistance, …"
   – Michel Foucault.

Hypatia (born 355 C.E. – died 415 Alexandria), philosopher, mathematician, and astronomer, who studied the night sky, is also one to have said it is important to "reserve the right to think." She is famous for her brutal murder by a group of men, most of them monks.

Hypatia was the daughter of the mathematician and astronomer Theon of Alexandria, and the last member of the Alexandrian Museum. Theon's work involved preserving Euclid's Elements, his writings on Ptolmey's *Almagest and Handy Tables. The Almagest is a surviving work from the ancients on astronomy.* Hypatia continued this preservation of Greek mathematical and astronomical heritage, credited with an astronomical table, Apollonius of Perga's Conics and Diophantus of Alexandria's number theory *Arithmatic. Hypatia's significant work in algebra; she wrote commentary on the Arithmetica of Diophantus in thirteen books. Diophantus, called "the father of algebra," lived and worked in Alexandria in the 3rd century. He developed indeterminate equations.*

The Almagest by Ptolemy [69]

Well do I know that I am mortal, a creature of one day.

But if my mind follows the wandering path of stars

Then my feet no longer rest on earth, but standing by

Zeus himself, I take my fill of ambrosia, the food of the gods

---

[69] Ptolemy, 2nd century. Ptolemy's Almagest. London: Duckworth. 1984.

Hypatia was the leading astronomer and mathematician of her time, and the leading philosopher lecturer of Alexandria. Her philosophy was Neoplatonist, concerned with the One, an underlying reality accessible from the platonic forms.

Hypatia was a pagan and a brilliant woman at a time of complicated political and religious conflict. Then those had to believe the official "it" or else. Hypatia taught Neo-Platonism (appeared in the 3rd century); her philosophy was intellectual (unity, intelligence, soul) interpretations vary but the intellectual Neo-Platonism was not necessarily shut down because it did not conflict with Christianity. In other words, the pagans and religious alike listened to her lectures.

The story goes that after a temple was raised in honor of the Greco-Egyptian god

Serapis, by Theophilus (Alexandria's bishop until his death in 412, who was also a friend of Synesius, an admirer of Hypatia's work), Hypatia could pursue her intellectual studies unimpeded. The temple of Serapis may have housed some of the texts from The Library of Alexandria, as well as Hypatia's works. With the death of these two supporters, the climate changed with the succession of Cyril as bishop in Alexandria, and Hypatia (as well as

the temple) became a
focus of intolerance.

Hypatia became victim
of a brutal murder by a
band of Christian
zealots. Socrates
Scholasticus writes how
Damascius says "many
close packed ferocious
men, truly despicable,
fearing neither the eye
of the gods nor the
vengeance of men …
rushed at her and killed
her."[70] [71]

---

[70] Socrates Scholasticus: The Murder of Hypatia (late 4th century). From Ecclesiastical History. Book VI. Ch. 15.

[71] See the illustration by Louis Figuier from *Vies des savants illustres, depuis l'antiquité jusqu'au dix-neuvième siècle* from 1866. Public Domain.

Socrates Scholasticus has another description: "Some of them, therefore, hurried away by a fierce and bigoted zeal, whose ringleader was a reader named Peter, waylaid her returning home and, dragging her from her carriage, they took her to the church called Caesareum, where they completely stripped her, and then murdered her with tiles. After tearing her body in pieces, they took her mangled limbs to a place called

Cinaron, and there burnt them."[72]

As a philosopher, a free thinker, and as a woman, Hypatia was a threat to the order. Scholasticus said "She explained the principles of philosophy to her listeners, many of whom came from a distance to hear her." She wore a philosopher's cloak which was a male garment. The city of Alexandria loved her and attended her lectures.

---

[72] Socrates Scholasticus: The Murder of Hypatia (late 4th century). From Ecclesiastical History. Book VI. Ch. 15.

> She was respected and
> admired, part of the
> community and
> committees.
> She remained unwed.

42. Hypatia's texts.

43. In Michel Foucault's
    "Method,"[73] Foucault
    reminds the reader that
    power is "not something
    that is acquired, seized,
    or shared, something
    that one holds on to
    or allows to slip away;
    power is exercised from
    innumerable points, in
    the interplay of

---

[73] *The History of Sexuality.*

nonegalitarian and mobile relations" (History of Sexuality). Power functions as a matrix of institutions, apparatuses, conventions, and mobilities. Power relations are intentional and can be destructive if closed to alterity, sexism and racism are a dangerous way.

44. Hypatia, notable woman in mathematics, astronomy, and philosophy, of northern Africa, in Alexandria,

Egypt, knew of the violence exerted by mobilities of power.

Hypatia, again, famous for exerting the right to think, having said: "reserve your right to think."

Hypatia's performance as a writer and mathematician must have threatened some of the, as Foucault wrote, "nonegalitarian power relations" around her by her being seen as unworthy as a subject in statehood as an "unrecognizable" in accordance with the intersections of religious and gender power relations around her.

45. In *Gender Trouble*, Judith Butler examines how "There is no gender identity behind the expressions of gender; ... identity is performatively constituted by the very "expressions" that are said to be its results" (Gender Trouble, p.25). In other words, gender is what one does rather than an essentialism;

gender is performative.
This is a freeing idea
from conformity of
gender expectations,
strict script roles.

46. Daesthetics - breaking
open judgements in a
performativity of texts.
Hypatia's performance
as a scholar hit a wall of
judgement in a sea of
tiles and oyster shells.
(As it was a band of
monks who drug her
into the street and killed
her) …

Hypatia's performance
of a text – a living text,

one who studies the sky
and ponders the
unknowable, challenged
the totalized judgements
of her time – fascism
led to her execution in a
closed climate of
political impossibility,
a lack of hospitality for
her ideas and identity.
The danger of
totalized judgements
with unchecked power
can lead to an
impossible death by
ignorant mob.
Impossible because the
ignorance is completely
closed to her
positionality, humanity.

What would happen
if the mob said, yes,
Hypatia lives here too,
and she has the right to
think. Hypatia argued
to reserve the right to
think, even if one is
"wrong."

Hypatia's murder is an
example of the
hegemonic powers "at
odds" with her
positionality – what was
considered "legitimate"
and "dominate" cast
her off as inhuman, not
worthy of life as an
author, astronomer,
philosopher, teacher, a
woman scientist, one
who dared to question

the sky and those under it.

47. Hypatia, the author of "The Astronomical Canon."

In memoriam

Double Entries: She was called a heretic, and murdered by a fanatical mob with tiles, as Socrates Scholasticus describes the event in the late

4th century:

> "Yet even she fell a victim to the political jealousy which at that time prevailed. For as she had frequent interviews with Orestes, it was calumniously reported among the Christian populace that it was she who prevented Orestes from being reconciled to the bishop. Some of them, therefore, hurried away by a fierce and bigoted zeal, whose ringleader was a reader named Peter, waylaid

her returning home and, dragging her from her carriage, they took her to the church called Caesareum, where they completely stripped her, and then murdered her with tiles. After tearing her body in pieces, they took her mangled limbs to a place called Cinaron, and there burnt them."[74]

Hypatia, a pagan, dragged through the streets unto her death at a Church, "for being

---

[74] Medieval Sourcebook. Socrates Scholasticus: The Murder of Hypatia (late 4th century). From Ecclesiastical History. Book VI. Ch. 15.

a heretic," where her clothes were torn off and she was then murdered with tiles and oyster shells, and burned. Her death marks a death of thinking through the execution of her body and shutdown of her texts in a historical moment. A murder of her body, her books.

Her body of work is a palimpsest violent scrambling of time and text, an execution, a murder of manuscripts. The text is torn asunder, scraped to death with oyster shells, and what blood also contaminates the memory of the text? Her death marks a historical erasure and the order to decimate the manuscript of her body of work.

After her death, the story goes that the Library of Alexandria was raided, and her writings were destroyed.

In the early 16th century, the famous Italian painter Raphael (1483-1520) wanted to honor Hypatia by including

her in the famous
philosophers painting
The School of Athens.
The Bishop of Rome
disproved of including
her, since she had been
killed by Christian
monks of Alexandria for
her "heretical teachings."
Raphael was unwilling
to give her seat up, so
he disguised her by
lightening her skin color
to look like a favored
nephew of the Pope.

Her portrait is a
metaphoric palimpsest
text in the making, a
disguise, a problem of
performance:

Hypatia, notable philosopher.

*Hypatia, a notable woman of philosophy, astronomy, and teaching, is also awarded a place setting at the dinner table of Judy Chicago.[75]

---

[75] See Judy Chicago. *Drawing for Hypatia Illuminated Letter on runner*, 1977. Mixed media on paper, approx. 9 × 12 in. (22.9 × 30.5 cm).

[76] Coatilcue

Coatilcue, or "skirt of snakes" is the Aztec Goddess who gave birth to the moon, stars, and Huītzilōpōchtli. Mother of the gods, the moon, sun, and stars.

---

[76] 5

Chapter 7:

On Painting: Artemisia Gentileschi.

A daesthetics in painting

54. Dasethetics in Painting. Warning: discussion of gender-based violence. Historical lacunae. Women and people of color, even as artists, have been marginalized historically. Many people cannot name even a few women painters working before 1900. Though there

were great ones, like the Italian painter Artemisia Gentileschi.
b.1593-1652/53.
Rome, Italy.
Italian Baroque painter, follower of Caravaggio, whom she worked with in Italy in the early 17th century.
Artemisia Gentileschi was the daughter of celebrated painter Orazio Gentileschi, who saw her talent. Her father hired a teacher to work with her, Agostino Tassi.

Rape, silencing, and shaming are forms of individual and systemic oppression that have an effect of systemic marginalization. Gentileschi was raped by Tassi in 1612. Gentileschi took Tassi to trial, in which Gentileschi was tortured by a sibille, thumbscrews, and cords of rope that pulled her hands while she was questioned, a torture device to determine whether a person told the truth. Each time she replied, "it is true." Over time, her reputation became linked with Tassi, which overshadowed her talent and branded her as "licentious."

She he is recognized as a feminist icon of painting. Her work paints women as active historical subjects.

Gentileschi painted her revenge into her oil canvases, with paintings depicting suffering and strong women from myth as well as heroines of history, like Judith. Here, on the following page, Artemisia stands as Judith, slaying Holofernes, represented as Tassi.

Image:

Gentileschi, Artemisia. Judith
Slaying Holofernes (1614–20)
Oil on canvas 199 x 162 cm
Galleria degli Uffizi, Florence.
By Permission of The
Ministry of Culture, Uffizi.
Image: Public Domain.

Image:

In Judith and her Maidservant, Judith stands as proud victor, in a heroic pose, while the head of Holofernes, lies in a basket. Painted a year after Gentileschi testified in a rape trial.

In 1616, Gentileschi was the first woman to be accepted in the Florentine Academy of Fine Arts, where she is held in high regard. Her work presents sociohistorical time – her art inscribed with the past – still visible in the present.

The Little Book of *Daesthetics* | 195

Artemisia Gentileschi presents herself as both a real person and as the personification of *La Pittura*. Iconographical Gentileschi may be recognized as *La Pittura* by the pendant around her neck, which alludes to imitation of art with the portrait. And Gentileschi can imitate the appearance of things well--she presents the viewer with a portrait of herself in the artist's imagination, in a personification of artistic genius.

Judy Chicago creates a place for her at The Dinner Party, with gold velvet fabric, symbolic of the "Artemisia gold" used in Gentileschi's paintings, with the layer around her plate to symbolize the place her father tried to create for her (Chicago, A Symbol of Our Heritage, 82). Art historian Mary Garrard writes how Artemisia Gentileschi "suffered a scholarly neglect that is unthinkable for an artist of her caliber"

(Garrard, Artemisia Gentileschi, 3).[77]
A daesthetic effect is Gentileschi's life work in a palimpsest of blue.

---

[77] Garrard, Mary D. Artemisia Gentileschi. Rizzoli Art Series. New York: Rizzoli, 1993.

Pentimento:
"The presence or emergence of earlier images, forms or strokes that have been painted over"

To paint over, the write over. This is not a pentimento

Chapter 8:

On a blue Daesthetics[78]

55a. Death and the Amatory

"Finite to fail, but infinite to venture."

– Emily Dickinson

A haunting: Timelessness[79] in philosophy, literature, and art the contemporary world can

---

[78] Blue paint; lament
[79] For more background on a deconstruction of timelessness, please text *On Leaving: Poetry, Daesthetics, Timelessness.*

be in life and death, the
ancient world, too,
knows this (of love, the
erotic, death, love, etc.).
The eternal (as a word,
permanent, frozen, and
fixed in space and time),
paradoxically endless,
continual, which implies
movement and trace
between presence and
absence, infinite, and
finite.
b. A contemporaneous
labyrinth. An eternal
return. The return which
doesn't seem to fully
arrive.

56. Doing Daesthetics: Timelessness is a poetics of infinite finitude, which implies motion and becoming in a play of différance. The poet and painter are double in time and space – the poet goes into the world of the dead, a finitude. To revive, spectral memory.

To remember is to incite the mind with a spark of life. As Georges Bataille reminds us in *The Tears of Eros*, it is "out of the awareness of death that eroticism appeared" – it could be said that memory is a memory of death, out of which the erotic emerges. To "double six" it. The orgasm remembers death in its celebration of life, of the rebirth of joy, the senses to life. Amour. Those who gave the name *la petite mort*, "the little death" or the "brief loss or weakening of consciousness," or "the sensation of post orgasm

as likened to death"[80]
might see the height of
life veiled in the
funeral event.

What is for Roland
Barthes as the experience
of reading great works of
literature, is the
"fainting fit" of 1572.

Georges Bataille writes
"the erotic moment is
given the zenith of this
life, in which the
greatest force and the
greatest intensity are
revealed…" (33).

---

[80] "petite mort" Oxford English Dictionary.
(Third Edition). Oxford University Press. 2005.

The greatest intensity being writhing overflow of life. That which "will soon doom them to the corruption of silence" is a moment of memory of life in its most live moment. And "indeed, to judge from appearances, eroticism is by all accounts linked to birth, to a reproduction that endlessly repairs the ravages of death" (Bataille, 33). This Dionysian frenzy of life staves off the memory of death. The "little death" is the death inscribed in the erotic, the awareness of the finite of life, the daesthetic[81] interlude. What is open at that moment is oneself, in this interplay of the little death. La petite mort is the suspended but brief liberation of death as pleasure.

What is palimpsestic[82] is the erotic scraped out of the text. Bataille writes how in casting the eroticism out of religion,

---

[81] Death, beauty of life
[82] Inscribed and reinscribed; erased or partly visible

religion was deduced
to mere moralism. It
is here that the erotic
was censored out in the
destruction of ancient
libraries in the burning
of Alexandria.
Dionysus, the god of the
feast, of ecstasy, Eros,
wine, and madness is
at least attempted to be
partially erased.

The Little Book of *Daesthetics* |209

57. The importance of Eros. The horrific role of totalitarianism – to condemn alterity, desire, spontaneity, the erotic, the "mad" frenzy of Eros. Paradise is delayed, deferred in the world of perceived order. The erotic was doomed to trickery, to diabolical demise and condemnation of the nude.

58. In the Middle Ages, to show nudity was to show the horror of the

nude, as in Thierry Bouts Hell or The Fall of the Damned (1400-1475). (Louvre). Opposite Page, Image 14. The body is "scraped out." The somatic text is destroyed.

Eroticism, Bataille said, "is the assenting to life up to the point of death"[83] because death "jerks us out of a

---

[83] Bataille. Eroticism: Death & Sensuality, 1957, p. ... 2;4.

tenacious obsession with the lastingness of our discontinuous being" (p. 4).

Heart extraction during Human sacrifice in the Codex Magliabechiano, Folio 70. The sacrifice was to the life of the sun, the light.

The Little Book of *Daesthetics* |215

Poem for Calling in
Mictēcacihuātl, for friends

To swallow the stars during the day-

Her role is to watch over the bones of the dead.

Healing and shelter into the afterlife… or the grave

Calling for protection from violence…[84]

Love, protection, strength, Eros alterity-utopian futurity[85]

---

[84] Santa Muerte
[85] Poem by author

The Little Book of *Daesthetics* |217

She is the
personification of
death.
Lady Death.
She has indigenous
roots, Mictēcacihuātl.

And the medievalists practiced human sacrifice, in a discriminatory way toward alterity, a way of trying to suffocate the erotic Eros. But Eros has a way of coming back. Eros and Thantos. Freud identifies two drives - Eros is the drive for creativity, life, love, sexuality, and self-satisfaction. Thantos, from the Greek word for "death" is the drive for destruction, aggression, violence, sadism, and death.

In Civilization and its Discontents, Freud says humans have invented the tools to exterminate themselves; in turn, Eros will assert "But who can foresee with what success and with what result?"

All these sacrifices of Eros in the medieval era did not make life more peaceful. Alterity cannot be extinguished.

Georges Bataille says: "eroticism is accenting to life, even in death."

Like lobsters kept alive
until dropped in
boiling water, the
painting "Hell"
condemns the "erotic"
and sense of the nude
body to death. Erotic
joy is shown in censure,
a continuous attempted
erasure of Eros… just as
violence to joy and
alterity has inflicted
unjustly.[86]

58b. The painting
surfaces with an
inscription of horror.
The daesthetic interlude
is the aesthetic of death

---

[86] Image 14: Dieric Bouts "Day of Judgement" (circa 1420-1475) [Public domain].

and the erotic inscribed within the finite, in this case with the torture of the nude in painting. "Hell" depicts the law of the time, the judgment of high treason, where bodies were dismembered, disemboweled, quartered and or burned at the stake - executed in public spaces.
The art of hell reflects the torture of the time.

Eros / desire was dangerous, and "Heresy" was a capital offense, punishable by burning or hanging. All the texts that were burned, all the bodies, the works, destroyed by an idea of mastery and punishment. A death of texts.

64. Aphra Behn
The confidence in the nude in art returns in the west with the risqué libertine, one who is affirmed in the return of the voice in drama and poetry.

17th century Aphra Behn...

Aphra Behn doubles the voice in Libertine poetry and Drama, exploring gender inequity, cross dressing, bawdy female characters, lesbianism, and challenges the censored erotic:

Aphra Behn

"Let's Ramble…"

The Dream

"All trembling in my arms Aminta lay, / Defending of the bliss I strove to take; / Raising my rapture by her kind delay, …"

65. Rebellion.

Olympe de Gouges
1748-1793.

Playwright, activist, abolitionist,

Essayist -

A passionate advocate for equal human rights

Her 1793 article "Les Trois Urnes" led to her arrest and execution.

Chapter 9:

Vanitas

59. Daesthetics and the Lobster: Jan de Heem's "Still Life with Lobster" (1643) depicts the dinner banquet of decaying food stuffs in the memento mori tradition.

The lobster, a delicacy (in 17th century Holland), is kept alive until dropped in boiling water.
The position of the glass, standing halfway on the jewelry box, seems to suggest an insecurity and fragility of life and time

itself, illustrating the Latin idea of nascendo morimur "we are born to die."

Vanitas paintings depict a view of the impermanence of life. We cannot take these things with us, or the ephemeral nature of earthly joy is fleeting, worldly wealth empty. Death eradicates it all.

In the Encyclopedia of Comparative Iconography, the skeleton as a memento mori is described as a symbol which appeared in the Middle Ages and the Renaissance associated with figures in northern European representations of the ars moriendi, *Dance of Death or totentanz (danse macabre).* In the sixteenth century the symbol of death was a skull. The Encyclopedia of Comparative Iconography says: "In the seventeenth century the symbolism of the memento mori expanded to include many emblematic objects in addition to the skull. Sometimes a portrait of the deceased was replaced by a skull as a new kind of painting emerged: vanitas still life paintings. As this theme expanded, the figure (portrait) re-centered vanitas painting and entire scenes became allegories on the transitory of human existence." [87]

---

[87] Liana de Girolami Cheney, "Vanity/Vanitas" in Encyclopedia of Comparative Iconography: *Themes Depicted in Works of Art*, vol 2, ed. Helen E. Roberts. (Chicago: Fitzroy Dearborn, 1998), 887.

> "Eroticism is accenting to life even in death"
>
> – Georges Bataille

59a. Palimpsestic Medieval recycling. Scrape manuscripts, to rub partially clean, and re-write. [88]

---

[88] Palimpsestic texts remain, such as the texts by ancient Romans who used wax tablets; the Codex Ephraemi Rescriptus 5th century Greek Old and New Testaments covered with works of Ephraem the Syrian 12th century (Bibliothèque nationale de France); Codex Nitriensis contain *The Iliad*, The Gospel of Luke (6th century) and *Euclid's Element's* 8th century (British Museum); and other works such as the Wolfenbüttel Codex (where the upper texts is 10-11th century, and lower is 6th), to name a few. *palímpsēstos*, from παλίν + ψαω = «again» + «scrape». Also: a genus of moth.

Image:

The Novgorod Codex unearthed in Novgorod, hyper-palimpsest text of three wooden tablets. Stratigraphy; dendrochronology dating 999. Wax codex of the 11th century and carbon dating to 999. Concealed texts.

59b. Daesthetics, an
aesthetic motif of nature
mort, the ephemeral
in sculpture, codex,
painting. To scrape; rub
smooth.

The Kiss of Death.
When Eros and Thantos Meet
Reader, look up this statue as you read on…
[89] El petó de la mort The Kiss of Death. Poblenou Cemetery. 1930.

---

[89] Sculpture reference: *The Kiss of Death.* Marble statue.

In this "death and the maiden"[90] motif painting the woman turns, and discovers, to her surprise, and horror, she is kissed by death. His hands grip her hair as he points to the grave as if to say, "your time is up." This death and the maiden motif evolved from the Danse Macabre. Look at the painting while listening to Franz Shubert's song "Der Tod und das Mädchen" or String Quartet no.14

---

[90] Image 21 and 22. Death and the Maiden (1518-1520) by Hans Baldung Grien. Public Domain.

A nighttime
composition,
they stand in
a cemetery.

In *The Tears of Eros*, Bataille writes about violence and how the carnal gets violated. The erotic, put to death in the medieval era, gets re-inscribed in Renaissance art while art lovers' interest in paintings of the nude again arise during the Renaissance.

The nude- considered the "timeless ideal" of humanity, is inscribed in *Death and the Maiden*, with the skeletal personified as death itself, and finitude in aesthetics of the nude female body as the lament. She is horrified and the weeping willow as to Ophelia's death scene – with long purples[91] all around her body.

In both *Death and the Maiden* paintings, the maiden is horrified by the visage of death, the finite, who, in a forced grip as foodstuffs, is to be consumed.

The Renaissance erotic in painting is charged

---

[91] Long purples: orchids, "dead men's fingers"; a phallic symbol of the Renaissance language of flowers.

with demise, the stolen
kiss of death, the
mauling of body subject.
One might even wish
she would turn and run,
to strike finitude out
of the frame. As in the
great mystery of
philosophy in Hamlet,
in this [kiss of death]
"what dreams may
come"?

The body is condemned
to decay as food for
worms. It is as if one
must "come to life" to
remember it or suffer

death, a kind of passive
ennui.

Death and the erotic
are a common theme of
painting: the nude
portrayed passively,
eros in a frozen state of
horror, represented as
appetite foodstuff for
the personified skeletal
form, the hungry
monster of death.

The body is the medium
of passing, of leaving.
The monster is monere,
a memory, a warning of
the death that is
inevitably to come.

This aesthetics, daesthetics of the *Death and the Maiden* illustrates an aesthetic of the body as full of vibrant life, but also a double bind in the decay of foodstuffs, as the body is a mere subject to decay, to be eaten and devoured by death – in this painting, imagined as the agent in grip, the great worm in control of passing life. Afraid of being eaten by the monster, consumed, to horror. The Maiden is a metaphor for the life of commerce, where the body is viewed as a subject to eat, even to the point of death.

In *Death and the Maiden*, the maiden might transform into a sheet of death. The cloth of the maiden is like flesh, she is passing and turning into the sheet, to cover her like parchment. The maiden is transmogrified into a pale white sheet that will wrap her body in the ground.

In *Death and the Maiden*, the warning of

violence and mortality
in a fear of the
encounter of violence is
personified as a monster.
She is food for the
appetite of
consumption, a
commerce of patriarchal
death capitalism. He will
consume her/them.

The death and the
maiden motif in
painting is a
palimpsestic[92] text in
passing.[93] A
daesthetics of the
ephemeral in painting.

---

[92] Hidden texts; death
[93] *Death and the Maiden* (1518-1520) by Hans Baldung Grien.

Vanitas is a work of art,
here a painting that
deals with the transience
of life and the certainty
of death. Vanitas art
also reveals the lacunae,
on what is missing:
one that alludes to the
passing, the fragility and
transience of life, in the
memento mori
tradition, *nature mort*).

Reviving the Dead:

60. Daesthetics and revival

O for Oosterwijck

Little is known about Maria van Oosterwijck's (1630-1693) vanitas paintings, which offer a glimpse into the absence of the body in painting; the flower flesh and skull with dark black backgrounds reveal the ephemeral; the fleeting. Denied membership in the painters' guild, as women were not allowed to join, despite her successful paintings and patronage, Oosterwijck devoted her life to work, to painting. She stands out as unique for her work.

The crowned skull is positioned to stare up at the sunflower, as if death is staring at life. The sunflower's sleepy head droops downward, as if to look at the bones. The fruit, half eaten, sits below the cut bouquet. A jewelry box sits to the left of the flowers and food, as if to suggest the love tokens will only remain. An open clock sits aside, as if left in haste. A letter lies below; all that is left to remain.

Vanitas motifs allude
to flowers, instruments,
decaying fruit, skulls,
music sheets, torn pages
of books. What can
be more transient and
fleeting than these time
pieces?

61. Daesthetics of Buoyant
    Time in Painting

As in Vanitas-Still Life
(1668) all that is left -
remnants of the human.
All what remains is
pleasure, the joys of life
– wine goblets, flowers,
sheet music, and a skull
amidst the decaying.
Wind music is
illustrated, a flute or
recorder. Stringed
instruments are often
depicted. Music is
transient, it is
momentary.

Drinking vessels are
overturned, as if left in
haste, to remind the

viewer of how fleeting life is. Especially life's pleasures, how quickly they disappear. Candles and sand clocks depict this disappearance, as do bubbles, butterflies, smoke – quick, fleeting images of the delicate nature of life. The skull, instruments of time, such as hourglasses symbolize a passing of time and death itself.

Daesthetics:

Art is an attempt to suspend death through image, substance.

Art is an uncertain attempt to capture the fleeting.

Annotation 62. Daesthetics as Enigma, time. Venus of Willendorf, c. 24,000-22,000 B.C.E., limestone 11.1 cm high (Naturhistorisches Museum, Vienna).

Kali, Sanskrit "she who is death"; Goddess of Death; Kala "time-doomsday-death." The Hindu Goddess of Death, Kali is Goddess of Time, Creation, and Destruction.

Kali is double agent: divine protector, one who bestows liberation, a bringer of destruction of harmful forces. She is the protector – her sword severs bondage, ignorance, ego.

Varma's chromolithograph shows well Kali's tongue ironically out reveling. In Cixous' "The Laugh of the Medusa," Cixous notes how using speech, French "voler" (both to fly; to steal) or the right to speak oneself and fly by will. [94]
[95]

---

[94] See Medusa's Terracotta antefix with the head of Medusa. 6th century B.C. Terracotta, Paint. Metropolitan Museum of Modern Art. Open access.

[95] See The Snake Goddess from Crete. 1600 B.C.E. See also Fresco from Pompeii, Casa di Venus. 1st century C.E.

63. Botticelli destroyed some of his work by fire after being preached to about religious reform.

The first monumental depiction of the nude goddess since ancient times: the famous Botticelli's Birth of Venus, an iconic image of the figure of Venus, the goddess of love, standing in a Renaissance painting.

Until this time in the Renaissance, the only time one would most

often see a nude in
Western art, it was Eve.
However, Venus here
is born of the sea and
stands on a seashell. The
(possible) impossibility
of the painting is one
where everything is
floating.

She has yet to be
clothed, the zephyrs
blow wind, the
attendance waits to
drape clothing on her.

An audience might
expect to see grounded
figures, clothed and

weighty, yet Venus seems
to float surpassing time,
elevated to a goddess
stature, as if the nude
wouldn't be condemned
to death. The fluttering
drapery and the
floating blossoms
suggest a movement,
suspension in time.
A timeless time.

This nude reveals the
birth of Venus in all her
glory; the celebration of
the birth of the goddess
from sea, where there is
no control. Gaia gave
Cronos a sickle. Cronos

castrated Uranus and threw his testicles into the sea, and out of the sea foam rose Aphrodite, bedazzled and "throned," as Sappho called her.

Cutting the Thread
See the Bas relief of Atropos cutting the thread of life. Atropos from ancient Greek is "without turn." The daughters of the night - Atropos is one of the three Moirai whose Roman equivalent is Morta.

Atropos ended the life of mortals and cut their threads. Her sister Clotho spun the thread and Lachesis measured the length.

Atropos bestows her name to the Atropa belladonna, or deadly nightshade, but also to the medicine atropine. She is a double agent, both poison and antidote as the pharmakon in Derrida's "Plato's Pharmacy."

"I like the dead,
they are the
doorkeepers who
while closing one
side give way to
the other."

                -Cixous

The Little Book of *Daesthetics* |273

Chapter 10:

Music, the Fleeting

66. Music, Daesthetics and the Ear

Music is transient. To read, to listen, to hear: the book (written text, the novel, the lyre's sheet music, etc.) in its written, musical form; music is punctuated wind, air. Jean-Luc Nancy wrote "music listens to itself." The reader can continue to read and hear the words of the dead writer, of

notes on air; the listener
/ reader can long for; to
communicate with the
ghost through the
double voiced
written text via music.
To touch the words if
one is blind; to hear or
see, the sensory
experience with words,
to hear the music of
language.

The reader can ask a
question, and the
answer, possibly a riddle,
in the enigmatic
written text of the
endless enigma. To read

this is to commune with the dead. Music is a lacunal hit between silence. Death and fecundity, ephemeral life.

2.a. Leave: to depart. To bid farewell.[96]

67. Suspend in air. Music. The contemporaneous motion of leaving is akin to death and time in textum,[97] in a freeplay of finitude (as a limited space, never stagnant,

---

[96] O.E.D. pp.776.
[97] The textum web of language; the web of life and of the dead; a double.

meaning always slips away); the affirmation: there is no space permanent, untouched, immobile, or timeless as fixed: everything is constantly moving, leaving, changing, and, to invoke a Derridean aporia: différance as time (defer, differ); eros, in life, in perishing.[98]

68. Deep unfathomable time has memory, memento mori,[99] in variation continuous, "passing from one state

---

[98] See Derrida's text *Aporias*.
[99] Memento mori: Latin for "remember that you will die."

to another." Even in leaving, how Derrida says "freeplay is the disruption of presence" – there is finitude disrupting, there is constant flux and motion, freeplay in language as a fading away in time.

69. Leaving is an Etymology: a communicative model of leaving one to another word in radical departures, freeplay. The signifier leaves the sign into a radical departure

from tradition, as can be seen in the deconstruction of the word "leave" in all of its variation.[100] (To go, to give, to die, to exit, to depart, to grow, to postpone, pages in a book, to postpone, ... etc).

70. Leave, Entry 14:
"a. leave behind.
(Also, to leave behind one).
(a) To neglect, leave undone (obs).
(b) not to take with one

---

[100] Variations of the word "leave" throughout this text; see also chapter two and subsequent chapters.

at one's departure, to go away without.
(c) to have remaining after departure or removal, as a trace[101] or consequence.
(d) to outstrip" (O.E.D., 778).

71. Daesthetics, Ontologies of Leaving[102]

72. "Daesthetics" or aesthetics of ontologies as a palimpsestic work of "leaving" in the fleeting. "Leaving" resists stable meaning, an onto-end.

---

[101] Derrida on trace.
[102] "Ontologies of Leaving" in *Poetry Daesthetics Timelessness* (2014) essay by the author.

73. What does this mean, to leave, in a sense of the lacunae? This line of thinking is toward an ontology of the lacunal "leaving." To leave implies a space which is not ontologically or metaphysically hierarchical; it is beside itself, in passing, after, yet continuous; a continual leaving; a passage, an aporia. A gap, lacunose, meaning many holes in the text. To remain is only temporary. Even to die is to remain only

temporarily, there is
perishing in/on the
earth, or in the mummy
wrap, the leaves of the
text remain in
fragments. The
proximity of space,
discontinuing;
paradoxically the Old
English, læfan[103] "to let
remain; remain; have
left; bequeath," …

74. Daesthetics as
leaving. Germanic root
is "to remain, continue;"
yet to depart; to retreat;
to die. Another
etymology of leaving is

---

[103] O.E. *læfan* (to leave, bequeath). A Guide to Old English, 6th edition.

quoted at length, and a decentering follows:

Leave (v) O.E. læfan "to let remain; remain; have left; bequeath," from P.Gmc. *laibijan (cf. O. Fris. leva "to leave," O.S. farlebid "left over"), causative of *liban "remain," (cf. O.E. belifan, Ger. bleiben, Goth. bileiban "to remain"), from root *laf- "remnant, what remains," from PIE *leip- "to stick, adhere;" also "fat." The Germanic root has only the sense "remain, continue," which also is in Gk. lipares "persevering, importunate." But this usually is regarded as a development from the primary PIE sense of "adhere, be sticky" (cf. Lith. lipti, O.C.S. lipet "to adhere," Gk. lipos "grease," Skt. rip-/lip- "to smear, adhere to." Seemingly contradictory meaning of "depart" (early 13c.) comes from notion of "to leave behind" (as in to leave the earth "to die;" to leave the field "retreat")[104]

75. (Chambers Dictionary of Etymology).
a. Permission asked for or granted to do something. To ask, beg, get, give, grant, have, obtain leave. By your leave (as in an apology, often ironically).[105]

---

[104] Leave 2. "Permission, consent. 1129 leve; developed from Old English *læfe,* leafe (before 900, in Alfred's translation of St. Gregory's *Pastoral Care*)... Old Saxon Orlof. Related to Love, Believe, Furlough" (Chambers Etymology, 585).

[105] O.E.D. pp.786.

I. To have remainder; to cause or allow to remain. Of a deceased person.[106]
b. Of things or conditions: to have remaining as a trace or consequence after removal or cessation.[107]

To leave is to leave a gap. Lacunose. If one could leave; "to let remain" the body remains, perishes[108]; to depart is "to leave behind" and of course,

---

[106] Ibid.
[107] Ibid.
[108] Derrida on perishing in *Aporias*.

"to die" or "retreat." Death, of course, is the continual other which cannot be determined. Isn't death indeterminate, yet paradoxically the end? It is the "possibility of impossibility" (Heidegger). One could follow Derrida's aporia, since this is a puzzle: "indeed the non-passage, which can in fact be something else, the event of a coming or of a future advent, which no longer has the form of the movement that consists in passing, traversing, or transiting".[109] Having "come to pass", always, "the aporia, that is, the impossible, the impossibility", that which "cannot pass [...] or come to pass",[110] the aporia might indeed attest to "the fact that the impossibility would be possible and would appear as such, as impossible, as an impossibility that can nevertheless appear or

---

[109] Derrida, J., *Aporias*, p.8.
[110] Ibid. P.23.

announce itself as such"[111] Levinas: "it is not with the nothingness of death, of which we precisely know nothing, that the analysis must begin, but with the situation where something absolutely unknowable appears. 73. Absolutely unknowable means foreign to all light, rendering every assumption of possibility impossible".[112] The

---

[111] Derrida, J., *Aporias*, p. 12.
[112] Levinas, E. (1989), "Time and the Other" (tr. by R. A. Cohen). In: E. Levinas, *The Levinas Reader* (ed. S. Hand), Oxford and Cambridge, MA: Basil Blackwell, p. 41 (pp. 37–58).

possibility of the impossible is the possibility of death; as leaving, as unknowable and also foreign, opening the possibility of entering different unknown terrains, foggy, unclear spaces and scenes. 74. À la recherche du temps perdu, "We say that the hour of death cannot be forecast, but when we say this we imagine that hour as placed in an obscure and distant future. It never occurs to us that it has any connection with the day already begun or that death could arrive that same afternoon, this afternoon which is so certain and which has every hour filled in advance" (Proust, Marcel). Proust illuminates through the paradox how the very "certainty" of the afternoon is contaminated by the uncertain, via the arrival of death as a sublime liminal threshold.

76. Toward an aesthetics of leaving and becoming a gap in fleeting time, a daesthetics. This daesthetics , a being-with finitude in language; a meditation on less time, a hospitality for mourning.

77. A hospitality for a daesthetic time-less-ness of leaving in musical variation. A musical space for the newcomer? An embrace. An elegy, a

eulogy. New friends? Is
it possible to
welcome the other, like
a musical
composition?
Hospitality, in
welcoming the other;
letting the other arrive,
to invite l'etranger on
a personal and political
level, which often is
a waiting,[113] needs a

---

[113] Caputo writes about how this raises socio-political questions "about refugees, immigrants, "foreign" languages, minority, ethnic groups, etc. Derrida's interest is drawn to the fact that, by virtue of its etymology, the word "hospitality" carries its opposite within itself (that's a surprise!). The word "hospitality" derives from the Latin *hospes,* which is formed from hostis, which originally meant "stranger" and came to take on the meaning of the enemy or "hostile" stranger (*hostilis*), + pets (*potis, potes, potentia*), to have power" (110). (Note: Derrida is referencing the

space for listening: (See Jean-Luc Nancy's work *Listening*).

"Music Listens to Itself"

-Jean-Luc Nancy

---

etymology of Emil Benveniste, in Le vocabulaire des institutions indo- Européennes I (Paris: Minuit, 1969), chap. 7, "L'hospitalité."

78.

> *Welcome the music! Let's hear the music of suffering.*[114] *Let's hear the lyre.*
>
> *- Sappho Fragment 42*
> *"Eros shakes my soul"*

```
"Without music,
life would be a
mistake"

        - Nietzsche
```

---

[114] Nietzsche reminds us that "…without music, life would be a mistake", something is missing-

"Music combines all qualities; it can exalt us, divert us, cheer us up, or break the hardest heart with the softness of its melancholy tones. But its principal purpose is to direct our thoughts toward higher things, to elevate and even to shake us…" (Liébert, Nietzsche and Music, p.18)

79. Music: Eros. The notes are out of reach, in flight. Desire is a suspended daesthetic, a punctum, a wounding

which strikes to feel
the pain and joy of life,
Amor Fati.

80. The desire to wait is a
desire for waiting for
oneself, to wait for the
other, to serve the other.
In what follows Derrida
explains the arrivant
vis-à-vis the threshold,
a leaving the home, a
hospitality for the other.

81. Is it possible to have a
hospitality for death of
a master in language to
serve the other? A, what
Derrida says is a "Cinder

as the house of being"? (23). The house of being, the body, a decomposition, of ash? The scraping of the body, the book of one's life.

82. Daesthetics. In musical terms, music is a language of air in time signature imperfect.

83. A caesura; the silent pause in poetry and music.

84. Daesthetics as the uncertain caesura.

85. Oblivion. Finitude is as an opening to our condition of oblivion; even of illusion and fantasy, of what Avital Ronell calls a "Stupidity"[115] before finitude, the time-less enigma, which haunts philosophy, art, existence. In other words, Ronell says that "…we are forced by the very nature of finitude, stupidity is what we share…" (*Stupidity*, 93).

---

[115] Avital Ronell's text *Stupidity*.

86. Waiting in Derrida: the "awaiting oneself, await oneself in oneself"; the waiting for the arrivant (for something else); and the waiting for each other is a hospitality of finitude, a remembrance in deep time of leaving (of waiting and leaving) and the unknown of finitude. Unconditional mourning and hospitality, together, are an aporetic possibility for the mark of a potentiality for an

ethical becoming – not of a doxa or duality, but of deep time in multiplicity, a deconstruction of language in radical alterity for an ethics of a hospitality to imperfection.

87. (A memento mori can be called upon here, in this era of forgetfulness of finitude, to inspire the poet and music in an elegy of remembrance). Time is less. To think with the finite is to think with the service

to the other in a desire for communication, a bridge to return.

88. A poetic dwelling in texts ~~in text. Keeping time.~~

~~89. Time~~

~~90. to keep time open~~
    ~~Temps~~

91. à deux temps rapide; à la blanche
    Alla breve

92. Open notes.
   ~~The natural notes on a wind , a string, without any human fingers.~~

~~92. Speeding up at a different tempo, to cut time.~~

93. Intermission
   Lacunae: An extended silence in Music.

– sheet music,
time lapse

Chapter 11

Post- scripts: Lacunal Language[116]

- lacunose knowledge and leaves/paper, language in the open.

94. Leave-over: to allow to remain for future use[117]

    "... it means precisely the non-fixing of such a signification: not, however, as the powerlessness to fix it,

---

[116] Deep time in finitude; aesthetics and politics; poetics of aperture.
[117] Leave, O.E.D. entry *e* pp.779.

but as the power to leave it open."

- Jean-Luc Nancy
A Finite Thinking

95. Poetic dwelling is a dwelling of finitude, a time-as-less, not as stasis, but flux; one which recognizes finitude and the power of creative generation in difference of the gap. The unknown.

96. An alterity of what is unknown in the gap.

The undecidable gap/
lacunose in the text,
pottery, music, arts.
The lack, gap, caesura
as undecidable. This
undecidability leaves
open the possibility of
dwelling in an interval
of deep time poetics of
language in aperture,
leaving the possibility
for fidelity (Badiou)
to an affirmation of
language alterity in the
making, a perpetual
motion in leaving[118] and
undecidability (Derrida,
Ronell) in hospitality

---

[118] Leaving as post-structural poetics.

(Derrida), for the "to come," language as a play (Derrida) of continuous alterity, in affirmation.

97. Lacunal leavings[119] open a hospitality for the other in a brutish world, poetics is a space, an aperture in language, which resists closure in totalized meaning. A resistance to totalitarian or fixed thought on what the lacunose may be. To

---

[119] Lacunal leavings as gaps in the texts; openings; holes; missing text.

guess, question, leaving it open to possibility.

Through timeless ambiguity of finitude, whether in difference, in opening time and space through intervals of the uncertain, to stand on the edge is to see death and that unknowability in the other. A mathematical Sublime.

98. Daesthetics: There is an intrusion in

writing, the puncturing
wounding of the pen.
Lacunal "Leaving"[120] in
language (in the open),
in its infinite relation of
being-with-in-finitude
deconstructs the house
in the thresholds – the
foundation is not
present, there is leaving,
there are
indeterminacies, finite
remembrances, gaps in
memory as lacunose.

99. time-less-ness,
being-with in less time,

---

[120] Lacunal leavings: gaps in the texts; aperture; missing text.

of deep time, of being, as Avital Ronell says in *Stupidity*, "stupified."[121]

100. Lacunal leaving - a remembrance for the other in a poetics of infinite possibility a leaving, a departure from totalization, closure, and judgment. A gap. Opening.

101. Difference, alterity, is a gesture towards an affirmation of poetic dwelling, a

---

[121] See Avital Ronell's important book *Stupidity*.

remembrance of the sea, one's finitude, in a return to oneself, a remembering of one's own alterity, and another's alterity, like the "hangman."[122]

102. The Latin translation for textum is web. Language, a lacunal web, a riotous multiplicity in continual duration, in time-less[123] flux, is inexhaustible, even in finitude. A web of

---

[122] suspension, suspension of knowing, suspend judgment.
[123] See previous chapters on time-less-ness, finitude, and poetics.

language, textum in the gaps of leaving, is timeless differance in alterity; even one's singularity, textum ad infinitum – in affirmation of gaps of knowing.

103. It is the memento mori, remembrance of finitude, and poetic aperture, infinite aporetics, which is vital to the sharing in re-opening, a poetics of deep time. For, determinism is not

sufficient to define poetics of language, in alterity, its time-less enigma, which resists totalized closures of the textum; an aperture of poetics, in lacunal leaving.

104. Time-less-ness and daesthetics is a media philosophy of leaving, which explores the existential deep time, through poetics of finitude, which illuminates the sublime magnitude of the

endlessness, the unfathomable, the "finite infinite."

105. Time-less-ness is illuminated in philosophical poetics of deceleration, the elegiac slow time, in a language of daesthetic philosophy of leaving, a deep time travel, in worm holes, apertures of dwelling. Becoming is of leaving, departure, elegiac leave-taking, the finality, the end, of death and becoming in leaving (of loam). In

other words,
becoming is an ontology
of change, of movement,
of flux, of daesthetic
"leaving."

106. To write is a "leaving."
The leaf. the pages of a
book, to pass, an aporia.

The Little Book of *Daesthetics* |319

"My heart's grown heavy, my knees will not support me/... This state I oft bemoan; but what's to do? / Not to grow old, being human, there's no way"

- Sappho, Book IV.

107. Daesethics: The task of translation.

107a. Re-reading Sappho: Time is scrambled and palimpsestic. Inscribed and re-inscribed such that the previous text is imperfectly erased and only partly visible, if not at all --through the lacunal gaps and worms of time.
A Moth.

108. Texts ordered to death. At what point is a manuscript ordered to death, executed? What

happens to its body, its voice, it's remains? Its entrails and blood?

109A. Remains. Sappho's poems are labeled as fragments and numbers in 20th-21st century translations. What remains today is the fragmentary voice of Sappho as a poet, who still haunts the reader, the palimpsestic[124] texts in translation.

109. Undecidables
The poet is a threshold

---

[124] metaphoric

of leaving into deep
time; the poet returns
from the dead and tells
their story.[125] Poetic
language has a potential
to disrupt and subvert
presence and
alacrity through deep
time between the
undecidable[126] spaces of
finitude, poetics, and
philosophy, which opens
language to a possibility

---

[125] Even in death, the writer speaks.

[126] Derrida. Note: the word undecidable will be used in this text, always referring to Derrida on the undecidable. Derrida writes how undecidables ". ... situate perhaps better than others the places where discourses can no longer dominate, judge, decide: between the positive and the negative, the good and the bad, the true and the false" (*Points*, p.86).

of an undecidable
intervals of flux in
language, but also an
aperture of deep time.
Time is less; there is
finitude.

110. Timelessness is unfixed,
indeterminate,
unfinished, a non-linear
aperture of leaving,
of finitude in
fecundity. There is an
interval between (art)
poetry language and
philosophy where a
space of indeterminism
ruptures into sublime

undecidability,[127] a magnitude of infinite mystery, an aporia into what is unknowability, otherness, such as of

---

[127] Avital Ronell; Jacques Derrida on undecidability. Derrida states, in his text *Deconstruction and the Possibility of Justice*: "The undecidable is not merely the oscillation between two decisions; it is the experience of that which, though heterogeneous, foreign to the order of the calculable and the rule, is still obliged – it is of obligation that we must speak – to give itself up to the impossible decision, while taking into account of law and rules. A decision that did not go through the ordeal of the undecidable would not be a free decision, it would only be a programmable application or unfolding of a calculable process" (24). It is important to note how the undecidable is not an "oscillation between two decisions" as Derrida emphasizes, but within every decision is an opening for indecision, as there is transformation and change.

death.[128] A mourning
for what has been lost.
Time.

111. V
Vanishing. Wind. An
interval of poetics and
philosophy is
time-less-death.
An elegiac opening in
finitude, is
indefinable and
undecidable,
non-linear and
indeterminate aporias in
deep time through the

---

[128] There is a haunting in the undecidable for Derrida. Finitude here is a place of indeterminate wonder, a space of "negative capability" (John Keats).

poetics of death as unknowability,[129] undecidability.[130] Timelessness is not fixed as it has been habitually claimed, but uncertain and indeterminate, unfinished, non-linear aperture of the leaving.

---

[129] Avital Ronell: on unknowability in *Stupidity*. Judgment is suspended: the individual is "stupid before the other" (66). Closure a judgment. Passing judgment is closure, a refusal or finality, is a metaphysical totalization conceptualization, which does not allow for alterity / singularity.
[130] Derrida, on the undecidable.

Chapter 12:

Lacunal Leaving, Moths

112. Lacunae. Leaving; to disappear; an opening, moving, in betwixt staying and another, between being-there and vanishing, a myopic blur, clouding and disrupting the illusory fixation of presence of time as static, absolute, eternal, presence. This motion renounces origin: it is continuously labyrinthine between memory and moment,

unfrozen, paradoxically finite.

113. The Exit. Timelessness is the interval of leaving,[131] of palimpsestic finitude and deep time in an aperture, a poetics of exit, the interval of rootlessness and departure in language under the knife.

114. There is no possession of time,[132] time is

---

[131] Leaving is used here as a wild card, of indefinite meanings. Leaving resists closure, opening.

[132] Siegfried Zielinski, in *A Trilogy of Time*, lectures on how one cannot lose time; there is no possession of time: "time has us." He explains the holy trinity of time (Past Present Future) in Transmediale.

constantly leaving, slipping away, exposing its own departure, exposing fragility and openness. Time comes and goes … (lacunae)

115. There is departure and rupture within the presence, there is play within disposal of the present, a leaving which ruptures into another, a threshold of becoming loam. 116. There is the "relinquishing" of art in the "disposal" and the

interplay of the flux of movement of time, in continuous movement. Like Derrida's pharmakon and his hidden hymen,[133] the etymology of "leave" is a wildcard in meanings, not of one definition or fixed into a presence

---

[133] See Derrida on the hymen. Derrida calls names: "paleonyms," and he also provides a list of these "old terms": "pharmakon"; "supplement"; "hymen"; "gram"; "spacing"; and "incision" (Derrida, Positions, p. 43). These names are aged because, like the words "appearance" and "difference," they have been used in the history of Western philosophy to refer to the "inferior position" in hierarchical dichotomies in a metaphysics of presence. But he uses them to refer to what has never had a name in "metaphysics"; they refer to that what is indeed "older" than the metaphysical judgment.

or absence (to leave: to "give"; to "remain" and yet to "depart," to "die", to "postpone" "to bequeath," "a page in a book," et. al.).

117. There are endless, open potentialities in the rootless etymologies of "leave."

118. Etymology itself is a philosophy of deconstruction, in a riotous multiplicity of meanings in interplay, freeplay,[134] in textum word plays, interaction between.

---

[134] Derrida, J. See "Structure, Sign, and Play in the Discourse of the Human Sciences."

119. A-centered leaves[135] without origins or center,[136] "leaves" as choirs of a book, into a freeplay of fecundity and finitude, of "leaving" betwixt time and spacing of leaving.[137]

120. Daesthetics is the earth, ash, loam of texts like Sappho's fragments in disintegration, remnants of parchment – the seen and unseen at work. Sappho's texts, only

---

[135] See previous text On Leaving… (2014).
[136] Derrida on freeplay of the sign: "the center is no center."
[137] Even in death, there is movement, leaving, becoming (earth, ash, loam).

partially lost in time,
generate great power
with the life that
remains in them.

121. X for Halima Xudoyberdiyeva.

*"Oshiqlaring poyingga
gul otib ham bo'ldi,
Xilvatlarda labingdan
bol totib ham bo'ldi,
Va bu haqda kimlargadir
sotib ham bo'ldi,
Sen baribir
muqaddassan,
muqaddas ayol."*

122. Y. Daesthetics, lacunae
in manuscript form.
A decentering of the
interval between time
and space in language,
a poetics of finitude[138]
which resists closure in
an unnamable process of
thinking, in suspension
of judgment.
The spacing interval is a
spacing for a possibility
of deep time as
postponement, an
aperture of leaving, and

---

[138] See Derrida/John Caputo *Deconstruction in a Nutshell* "That opening breaks the spell of present closure, allowing the present to be haunted by ghosts" (154).

of deferral.[139] It is this
space between
language, a space of
infinite relation, which
finds an interval in
variantologies of
undecidability in time,
a leaving in continual
relativity…

123. Time and space open
in language to many

---

[139] Derrida on deferral. Différance as time *ad infinitum* (defer, postpone; to be unlike, unidentical); to differ, to defer. "différence". *Différance (to* différer means to defer and to differ. Words can never be fully what they mean, they appeal to additional words. Meaning is postponed, endlessly. Différance is in continual flux. In addition, on the trace: in *Speech and Phenomena*, Derrida discusses how the "now" is always finding middle; compromised by a trace (62).

contemporaneous places
in non-linear Time.
Time is the only thing,
as Zielinski states "which
cannot be possessed"
(Zielinski, Deep Time
and the Media).

124. In the visage of
finitude, this opens a
possibility for
thinking in fidelity,
a de-materialization, a
de-composition.
To think with
finitude in mind, leaving
the poetic interval of
departure, a constant
elegy of our world in the

remembrance, opens a possibility for a fidelity of trans-formation through language of unjudging, undecidablity, uncertainty, and to quote Derrida, "knowing not to know" (Derrida).

125. This is a resistance to totalitarianism through awareness of one's own finitude. Why be closed when there is only so much time.

126. Lacunal leaving is
a possible time-less-ness
(of the finite, fleeting).
Time is less, in leaving.
The gap remains.
And a poetics of
dwelling in the possible
(without judgment)
opens a deep time in
language, a hospitality
for an infinite thinking
without closure,
without a war against
the other in dualism,
lapses into a shutting
down to thinking.

127. The artist, the poet is,
a translator, a listener to

the other, to time itself. This "double hearing" is the recognition of observance, as a guest who leaves the hospitality of hearing open. To listen is hospitality to the other's alterity. A welcome to futurity of possibility in the open.

128. This aural dwelling opens a possibility for a leaving judgment in communication, an interval space of deceleration in language and time, leaving open

an aporetic interval of
alterity in hospitality
of remembrance of the
other. Of Hypatia.
A possibility of
refrain, of knowing "not
to know", or pausing to
think? What texts might
remain? What texts
might still exist without
the violent murder of
Hypatia, Olympe de
Gouges, and … and…

129. Waiting.

130. For Derrida, experience
is when it is deferred

(and experience is about "the wait" and is constantly changing).

131. In Derrida's *A Taste for the Secret*, he analyzes how the horizon is "attached" to the future traditionally "as the Greek word indicates, a limit…" (20-).

132. There are aspects of futurity that cannot be determined. What is waited for is awaited "without horizon" as open, indeterminate:

"Awaiting without horizon of the wait, awaiting what one does not expect yet or any longer, hospitality without reserve, welcoming salutation accorded in advance to the absolute surprise of the arrivant from whom or from which one will not ask anything in return and who or which will not be asked to commit to the domestic contracts of any welcoming power (family, state, nation, territory, native soil or blood, language, culture in general, even humanity), just opening which renounces any right to property, any right in general, messianic opening to what is coming, that is, to the event that cannot be awaited as such, or recognized in advance therefore, to the event as the foreigner itself, to her or to him for whom one must leave an empty place, always, in memory of the hope—and this is the very place of spectrality [i.e., ghosts]" (65).[140] Such a wait without end may or may never occur. A western ontological illusion of duality has privileged the presence of physical "being there," in the "now" with the present time, equated against an absence, finitude. The waiting, without measure, indeterminate, as memory, the double, spectral, with temporary

---

[140] Derrida, Jacques. *Specters of Marx: The State of the Debt, the Work of Mourning, & the New International*. Trans. Peggy Kamuf. London: Routledge, 1994.

intermissions. This is the gap. We all await death. Why not be open to the possibility of …the uncertain?

133. Daesthetics. Suspend judgment. This is also where readers) (can we) turn to Jacques Derrida on the unknowable and Avital Ronell: on unknowability in *Stupidity*. Judgment is suspended: the individual is "stupid before the other" (66). To be blind to the

experience of the other. In this myopic blindness, oblivion, it is impossible to completely know the other.

134a. Perhaps this is where narcissism comes to play in its delusion as a center. If non-violence is possible (Freud says it may not be) then is it possible to not have a kind of violation? Non-violence, a firm stance.

134b. Protect the library, the archives.

Derrida: "[The death drive] works to destroy the archive: on the condition of effacing but also with a view to effacing its own "proper" traces" (13-14).

Derrida wrote on the archive and Freud's analysis of the death drive:

"As the death drive is also, according to the words Freud himself most stressed, an aggression and a destruction drive, it

incites not only
forgetfulness,
amnesia, the
annihilation of memory,
as mnemé or
anamnesis, but also the
radical effacement of
that which can never
be reduced to mnemé
or to anamnesis, and of
which I would like to
speak tonight, that is the
archive, consignment,
the documentary or
monumental apparatus
as hypomnema,
mnemotechnical
supplement or
representative,

auxiliary or memorandum. Because the archive, if this word or this figure can be stabilized so as to take on a signification, is neither memory nor anamnesis as spontaneous experience, alive and internal experience. There is no archive without a place of consignment, without a technique of repetition and without a certain exteriority. There's no archive without outside. Allow me to stress this Greek distinction between mnemé or anamnesis on the one hand, and hypomnema on the other, a distinction which has occupied me at length elsewhere. The archive is hypomnetic."[141]

The archive is outside memory which aids memory.

135. On violence. In his seminal text Civilization and its Discontents, Freud details anxiety

---

[141] Derrida, Jacques, and Eric Prenowitz. *Archive Fever: A Freudian Impression.* Chicago: University of Chicago Press, 1996. Print.

between society and the individual. The hunt for freedom is contrasted by civilizations command to obey the rules. The appetite for sexual interaction, for instance – prohibitive laws are created which strive to hinder the individual from pursuing adultery, violence, etc. so possibility is restricted by law. The possibility of happiness is then also restricted by the law, in this context of total freedom; therefore, civilization is discontent. For Freud, there is a predisposition toward a tendency for sex, and a violent tendency toward sexual competitors and authority figures, as they barricade the path to pleasure. The infantile need for the father's protection is then a most base need connected to an oceanic feeling of limitlessness, also associated with religion in cultural practices. So, then the explanation goes onto how this is partly why people are neurotic: they cannot tolerate what society imposes upon them as cultural rules and ideals. Is it possible to have non-violence if there is also desire?[142] This is a point to question a desire imposed upon another.

136. Eros, Desire.

137. Time is the lacunae.

---

[142] Avital Ronell and Judith Butler 2013 seminar at The European Graduate School on Freud's *Civilization and its Discontents*.

138. George Bataille, the awareness of death (the little death and eroticism) is one where "the identity of perfect contraries, divine ecstasy and its opposite, extreme horror" – he saw together in images of torture this paradox of the sexual and horror. One could turn to Freud for an engagement in this paradoxical view of the finite and horror. In Freud's "If we are to take it as a truth that knows no exception that everything living

dies for internal reasons – becomes inorganic once again – then we shall be compelled to say that *'the aim of all life is death'* and, looking backwards, that inanimate things existed before living ones' (Freud, 246, emphasis in the original).

139. Nietzsche's eternal return, the mind is connected to the material world in poetic sensibility. The eternal return into leaving,[143] ...

---

[143] *See On Leaving: Poetry, Daesthetics, Timelessness.*

140. In remembrance.

141. Still waiting.

142. Levinas: embrace the stranger; in remembrance.

143. To be spontaneous. The importance of spontaneity. See Hannah Arendt on the importance of spontaneity in The Origins of Totalitarianism.

144. The importance of Derridean hospitality.

145. Daesthetics as understanding the other in a place of finitude.

146. Daesthetics as poetic hospitality of alterity.

    "An act of hospitality can only be poetic."

    – Jacques Derrida

147. The undecidable - an alterity of language, the poetic

148. Derrida offers a perspective in which

language, in flux, is
freed from the confines
of chained metaphysical,
disciplinary opposition:

"Nevertheless, the
center also closes off the
freeplay it opens up and
makes possible. Qua
center, it is the point at
which the substitution
of contents, elements,
or terms is no longer
possible. At the center,
the permutation or
the transformation of
elements (which may
of course be structures
enclosed within a

structure) is forbidden. At least this permutation has always remained interdicted (I use this word deliberately). Thus, it has always been thought that the center, which is by definition unique constituted that very thing within a structure which governs the structure, while escaping structurality. This is why classical thought concerning structure could say that the center is, paradoxically, within the structure and outside it. The center is at the

center of the totality,
and yet, since the center
does not belong to the
totality (is not part of
the totality), the totality
has its center elsewhere.
The center is not the
center" (278-279).[144]

149. The center is decentered
in an opening, an
alterity.

150. Haunts on Repeat:
Avital Ronell; Jacques
Derrida on
undecidability.

---

[144] Jacques Derrida, *Writing and Difference*, trans. Alan Bass. London: Routledge, pp 278-294.

151. Derrida states, in his text Deconstruction and the Possibility of Justice: "The undecidable is not merely the oscillation between two decisions; it is the experience of that which, though heterogeneous, foreign to the order of the calculable and the rule, is still obliged – it is of obligation that we must speak – to give itself up to the impossible decision, while taking into account of law and rules. A decision that

did not go through the ordeal of the undecidable would not be a free decision, it would only be a programmable application or unfolding of a calculable process" (24). It is important to note how the undecidable is not an "oscillation between two decisions" as Derrida emphasizes, but within every decision is an opening for indecision, as there is transformation and change, a possibility for understanding or compassion.

152. There is a haunting in the undecidable for Derrida. Finitude here is a place of indeterminate wonder, a space of "negative capability" (John Keats). See Avital Ronell: on unknowability in Stupidity. Judgment is suspended: the individual is "stupid before the other" (66). Closure a judgment. Passing judgment is closure, a

refusal or finality, is a
metaphysical
totalization
conceptualization,
which does not allow for
alterity / singularity.

Derrida, on the
undecidable.[145]

---

[145] Notation: Derrida, "the metaphysics of presence" and Logocentrism: the word/Reason. "Logocentric – that which is centered on the "Logos" (= speech, logic, reason, the Word of God) - is the term used by Derrida to characterize any signifying system governed by the notion of the self-presence of meaning; i.e. any system structured by a valorization of speech over writing, immediacy over distance, identity over difference, and (self-presence over all forma of absence, ambiguity, simulation, substitution, or negativity" (Dissemination, 4). Platonic Forms are called "eternal patterns" (on an "original" and copy in Plato's Republic). Heidegger insists that western philosophy has privileged that which is / appears. Derrida writes in Limited,

Inc: "The enterprise of returning 'strategically', 'ideally', to an origin or to a priority thought to be simple, intact, normal, pure, standard, self-identical, in order then to think in terms of derivation, complication, deterioration, accident, etc. All metaphysicians, from Plato to Rousseau, Descartes to Husserl, have proceeded in this way, conceiving good to be before evil, the positive before the negative, the pure before the impure, the simple before the complex, the essential before the accidental, the imitated before the imitation, etc. And this is not just one metaphysical gesture among others, it is the metaphysical exigency, that which has been the most constant, most profound and most potent" (236). According to Derrida in Margins of Philosophy, metaphysics involves hierarchies of dualism and subordination (195). Difference is a "Derridean neologism combining the two senses of the French verb differer – "to differ" and "to defer or postpone" – into a noun designating active non-self presence both in space and time" (Dissemination, 5). An opening of desire.

153. Freud: ("I had to take detours")[146] A detour from -

154. Another bifurcation. And another.

155. Daesthetics as Nefelibata: (n). Lit. "Cloud Walker", from ancient Greek néphos (cloud) and latin (nebula); bátēs, "walker"; as
1. Daydreamer.
2. One who does not follow conventions.

---

[146] Avital Ronell, quoting Freud in Judith Butler & Avital Ronell's seminar session on Freud and Non-violence.

Daesthetics. Nefelibata: "one who lives in the clouds of their own imagination or dreams, one who does not obey the conventions of society, literature, or art."

156. Derrida: "The absence of the transcendental signified extends the domain and the interplay of signification ad infinitum" (Writing and Difference, 280).[147]

---

[147] Jacques Derrida, *Writing and Difference*, trans. Alan Bass. London: Routledge, pp 278-294.

157. Daesthetics, a lacunal leaving:[148] to postpone.[149]
To leave is to "postpone." Leave. b. "To allow to stand over, to postpone (an action, a subject of consideration)" (777).[150]

---

[148] Gaps in language; in the text itself; time lapses; missing text

[149] Derrida on deferral. Différance as time *ad infinitum* (defer, postpone; to be unlike, unidentical); to differ, to defer. "différence". *Différance (to* différer means to defer and to differ). The a is deliberate (what is written is not heard, which subverts the privilege of speech over writing). Words can never be fully what they mean, they appeal to additional words. Meaning is postponed, endlessly. Différance is in continual flux. In addition, on the trace: in *Speech and Phenomena*, Derrida discusses how the "now" is always finding middle; compromised by a trace (62).

[150] Oxford English Dictionary p.777.

According to philosopher Wolfgang Schirmacher on Derrida, the importance of keeping in the open is to:

"Postpone your judgment- the first lesson. Easy to say, nearly impossible to do, at least as a purely theoretical act. Therefore, it must be done without permission, not defended in discursive terms, just lived through"

– Wolfgang Schirmacher ("What If? A Tribute to Jacques Derrida")

158. To think daesthetically is to postpone, to double up.[151]

---

[151] In my book *On Leaving* (Atropos Press, 2014), the emphasis on postponing in relation to time and deferral: To leave is to postpone, a deferral of / in time. In *Speech and Phenomena*, Derrida explains how phenomenology is another illusive "metaphysics of presence" because it relies upon an enduring *self-presence*, (or in the case of Husserl, the possibility of an exact internal adequation) with oneself (*Speech and Phenomena*, 66-8). Derrida contests this valorization of an undivided subjectivity, as well as the primacy that such a position accords to the

159. Postpone judgement;
the question in the open
for thinking again and
again.

'now', or to some other kind of temporal immediate now. For instance, in *Speech and Phenomena*, Derrida argues that if a 'now' moment is conceived of as draining itself in that event, (as time speeds on)... it could not actually be experienced, for there would be nil to contrast itself against in order to clarify that very 'now' moment (passing time). Derrida clarifies in *Speech and Phenomena* how every supposed 'present', or 'now' point, is always already tainted by a trace, or a residue of *a past experience*, that prohibits us ever being in a *self-contained 'now' moment* (*Speech and Phenomena*,68). Following this repudiation of Husserlian temporality, Derrida remarks that "in the last analysis, what is at stake is... the privilege of the actual present, the now" (*Speech and Phenomena*, 62-3). Instead of emphasizing the presence of a subject to themselves (ie. the so-called living-present), Derrida strategically develops a conception of time that emphasizes deferral.

160. What is Daesthetics?
 Daesthetics is a
 Question.
 The Question is a
 movement of thinking.

161. A plasticity in reading.

162. The liminal. "Of or
 pertaining to a
 threshold. Latin, limen
 meaning" threshold,
 cross piece, sill." The
 betwixt.

163. To ponder, to
 question. The question
 can resist
 totalitarianism

b. sometimes in a Socratic way, to "live a life worth living," in and with questions. To question everything imaginable.

164. With the question… what possibility opens?

165. To take a leap.

166. Nothing.

1001. To postpone – this finitude and daesthetics of time, always in flux, to continue to wait for the future with finitude,

a future where the
possible, impossible
palimpsest text remains
to be ~~seen.~~
~~An aporia lost in time,~~
~~or destroyed.~~

~~1001+ to rise from the~~
~~ashes; to haunt.~~
~~E. escape.~~

~~1001+ Lacunae: Moths,~~
~~Bookworms, Foodstuffs.~~
~~Worm holes.~~

Moððe word fræt[152]

---

[152] Anonymous. The author's translation: "A Moth ate words." *A bug devoured song*s. Riddle 47. *Exeter Book*.

The Little Book of *Daesthetics* |377

Acherontia atropos[153],
A Death-Moth[154]
Acherontia Atropos
moth, the death's-head
moth ...

...10001+. Daesthetics.
The Incomplete
Monsters.

<u>Daesthetics as Post-Scripts.</u>

---

[153] Side Moth, not here. Acherontia Atropos gets its name from relating to death subjects. A. Atropos has a skull marking. The species Atropos relates to death and the goddess Atropos, one of the three Moirai.

[154] "Nor let the beetle, nor the death-moth be / your mournful Psyche, nor the downy Owl" – John Keats (Ode on Melancholy)

References:

Ahmed, Sara. *The Cultural Politics of Emotion*, by Sara Ahmed, NED - New edition, 2 ed., Edinburgh University Press, Edinburgh, 2014, pp. v-v. *JSTOR*, www.jstor.org/stable/10.3366/j.ctt1g09x4q.2. Accessed 18 Feb. 2020.

A Latin Dictionary. Founded on Andrews' edition of Freund's Latin dictionary. revised, enlarged, and in great part rewritten by. Charlton T. Lewis, Ph.D. and. Charles Short, LL.D. Oxford. Clarendon Press. 1879.

Barthes, Roland. *Camera Lucinda: Reflections on Photography*. Trans. Richard Howard. 1981. New York: Noonday. 1981.

Bataille, Georges. Erotism: *Death & Sensuality* / Georges Bataille; Translated by

Mary Dalwood. First City lights edition., City Lights Books, 1986.

Bataille, Georges. *The Tears of Eros*. City Lights Books, 1988.

Blanchot, Maurice. *The Instant of My Death*. Trans. Elizabeth Rottenberg. Stanford: Stanford UP, 2000.

Botticelli, Sandro. The Birth of Venus (c.1486). Tempera on canvas. 172.5 cm x 278.9 cm. Uffizi, Florence.

Butler, Judith.

> *Excitable Speech: A Politics of the Performative* (Routledge, 1997).
>
> *The Psychic Life of Power: Theories of Subjection* (Stanford University Press, 1997).
>
> *Feminist Contentions: A Philosophical Exchange*,

co-authored with Seyla Benhabib, Drucilla Cornell, and Nancy Fraser (Routledge, 1995).

Bodies that Matter: On the Discursive Limits of "Sex" (Routledge, 1993).

Feminists Theorize the Political,

with Joan W. Scott (Routledge, 1992).

Gender Trouble: Feminism and the Subversion of Identity (Routledge, 1990).

Subjects of Desire: Hegelian Reflections in Twentieth Century France (Columbia University Press, 1987).

What's Left of Theory? - New Work on the State and Politics of Literary Theory by Judith Butler, John Guillory, & Kendall Thomas (Routledge, 1999)

Caputo, John D., and Jacques Derrida. *Deconstruction in a Nutshell: A Conversation with Jacques Derrida.* New York: Fordham University Press, 1997.

Carson, Anne. *Eros the Bittersweet*. Champaign: Dalkey Archive Press. 1998. Print.

Cheney, Liana de Girolami. "Vanity/Vanitas" in Encyclopedia of Comparative Iconography: Themes Depicted in Works of Art, vol 2, ed. Helen E. Roberts. (Chicago: Fitzroy Dearborn, 1998), 887.

Critchley, Simon. The Book of Dead

Philosophers. NY: Vintage Books. 2008.

_____. The Ethics of Deconstruction: Derrida and Levinas. Edinburgh: Edinburgh University Press, 1999.

Codex Exoniensis: A Collection of Anglo-Saxon Poetry, from a Manuscript in the Library of the Dean and Chapter of Exeter, ed. and trans. by Benjamin Thorpe

(London: Society of Antiquaries, 1842. Derrida, Jacques,

_____*Adieu to Emmanuel Levinas*, trs., Michael Naas and Pascalle-Anne Brault, Stanford: Stanford University Press, 1999.

_____*Aporias*, tr., Thomas Dutoit, Stanford: Stanford University Press, 1993.

_____ *Archive Fever: A Freudian Impression*. Chicago: University of Chicago Press, 1996. Print.

_____Cinders. Ed. Ned Lukacher. University of Minnesota Press. 1991.

_____. *Demeure*. Fiction and Testimony. Trans. Elizabeth Rottenberg. Stanford: Stanford UP. 2000.

Dissemination, tr., Barbara Johnson, Chicago: University of Chicago Press, 1981.

_____*The Ear of the Other: Otobiography,*

Transference, Translation, tran. By Peggy Kamuf. "The Teaching of Nietzsche and the Politics of the Proper Name." Translated by Avital Ronell. New York: Schocken, 1985. pp.3-38.

_____*Edmund Husserl's Origin of Geometry: An Introduction*, tr., John P. Leavey, Jr., Lincoln, NE: University of Nebraska Press, 1989/1978.

_____ "Et Cetera," translated by Geoff Bennington, in *Deconstructions: A User's Guide*, edited by Nicolas Royle, London: Palgrave Macmillan, 2000, pp. 282-305.

_____ *Eyes of the University: Right to Philosophy 2*, Stanford: Stanford University Press, 2004.

_____ "Force of Law: The Mystical Foundation of Authority," tr., Mary

Quaintance, in *Deconstruction and the Possibility of Justice*, eds., Drucilla Cornell, Michael Rosenfeld, and David Gray Carlson, New York: Routledge, 1992, pp. 3-67.

_____. Geschlecht: sexual difference, ontological difference. *Feminist Interpretationf of Martin Heidegger*. Ed. Nancy Holland and Patricia Huntington. Penn. State University Press. 2001.

_____*Glas*, trs., John P. Leavey, Jr. and Richard Rand, Lincoln: University of Nebraska Press, 1986.

_____.
"Hostipitality" trans. Berry Stocker and Forbes Morlock. *Angelakai* 5:3. (December 2000).

_____*Limited Inc*, tr., Samuel Weber, Evanston: Northwestern University Press, 1988 [1977].

_____*Margins of Philosophy*, tr., Alan Bass, Chicago: University of Chicago Press, 1982.

_____*Memoirs for Paul de Man*, trs., Cecile Lindsay, Jonathan Culler, and Eduardo Cadava, New York: Columbia University Press, 1986.

Derrida, Jacques. *Monolinguism of the Other*, tr., Patrick Mensah, Stanford: Stanford University Press, 1998.

———"Nietzsche and the Machine: Interview with Jacques Derrida" (interviewer Beardsworth) in *Journal of Nietzsche Studies*, Issue 7, Spring 1994.

———. *On Cosmopolitianism and Forgiveness*. London and NY: Routeledge. 2001.

———.*Of Grammatology*, tr., Gayatri Spivak, Baltimore: The Johns Hopkins University Press, 1976.

_____.*Of Hospitality: Anne Dufourmantelle Invites Jacques Derrida to Respond*, tr., Rachel Bowlby, Stanford: Stanford University Press, 2000.

_____.*On the Name*, ed., Thomas Dutoit, Stanford: Stanford University Press, 1995.

Derrida, Jacques. Continued:
_____.*Of Spirit*, tr., Rachel Bowlby, Chicago: University of Chicago, 1989.

_____.*Of Sprit – Heidegger and the Question*, trans. G. Bennington and R. Bowbly, The University of Chicago Press, Chicago and London, 1989.

_____. *On Touching – Jean-Luc Nancy*, tr., Christine Irizarry, Stanford: Stanford University Press, 2005.

_____.*Paper Machine*, tr., Rachel Bowlby, Stanford: Stanford University Press, 2005.

_____.*Philosophy in the Time of Terror: Dialogues with Jürgen Habermas and Jacques Derrida*, ed., Giovanna Borradori, Chicago: University of Chicago Press, 2003.

_____.*Points ... Interviews, 1974-1994*, trans., Peggy Kamuf and others, Stanford: Stanford University Press, 1995.

_____.*Politics of Friendship*, tr., George Collins, London: Verso, 1997.

_____.*Positions*, tr., Alan Bass, Chicago: University of Chicago Press, 1981.

_____.*Research in Phenomenology* "On Reading Heidegger," #17: p.177.

_____. *The Postcard from Socrates to Freud and Beyond*, tr., Alan Bass, Chicago: University of Chicago Press, 1987.

_____. "Sending: On Representation" Social Research, 49:2

(1982:Summer). pp.324.

_____. *Specters of Marx*, tr., Peggy Kamuf, New York: Routledge, 1994.

Derrida, Jacques. *The Beast and the Sovereign*, trans. Geoffrey Bennington (Chicago and London: University of Chicago Press, 2009), p. 108.

_____. *The Ear of the Other*. Trans. Avital Ronell. University of Nebraska Press. 1985.

_____. *The Gift of Death & Literature in Secret*. Trans. David Wills. Chicago & London: University of Chicago Press. 1999; 2008.

_____. *The Truth in Painting*, trans., Geoff Bennington and Ian McLeod, Chicago: University of Chicago Press, 1987.

_____. *Speech and Phenomena*, tr., David B. Allison, Evanston, IL: Northwestern University Press, 1973.

_____. *Spurs Nietzsche's Styles*. Chicago: University of Chicago Press. 1979.

_____. *Without Alibi*, edited, translated, and with an introduction by Peggy Kamuf, Stanford: Stanford University Press, 2002. (The French versions of many of these essays can be found in *Jacques Derrida*, edited by Marie-Louise Mallet et Ginette Michaud. Paris: Editions de l'Herne, 2004.)

_____. *The Work of Mourning*, eds., Pascale-Anne Brault and Michael Naas, Chicago: University of Chicago Press, 2001.

_____. *Ulysses Gramophone: Hear Say Yes in Joyce.* Acts of Literature. Ed. Derek Attridge. NY: Routledge, 1992.

_____. *Writing and Difference*, tr., Alan Bass, Chicago: University of Chicago, 1978.

Figuier, Lousi. Hypatia Illustration from *Vies des savants illustres, depuis l' antiquité jusqu'au dix-neuvième siècle* from 1866.

Foucault, Michel, Alan Sheridan, and Michel Foucault. *The Archaeology of Knowledge*. 1972. Print.

Foucault, Michel. {1975.} 1979. Discipline and Punish: The Birth of the Prison. New York: Vintage.

Foucualt, Michel. 1976. "Method." The History of Sexuality. Paris, France: Editions Gallimard.

Freud, Sigmund. (1991a) "Beyond the Pleasure Principle" in *The Essentials of Psychoanalysis: The Definitive Collection of Sigmund Freud's Writing*, trans. James Strachey, ed Anna Freud. London: Penguin Books.

Garrard, Mary D. *Artemisia Gentileschi.*

Rizzoli Art Series. New York: Rizzoli, 1993.

Gentileschi, Artemisia. Judith Slaying Holofernes (1614–20) Oil on canvas 199 x 162 cm Galleria degli Uffizi, Florence.

Gentileschi, Artemisia. Self Portrait as an Allegory of Painting (La Pittura). 1638-39.

Grose, Francis. A Classical Vulgar Dictionary. 1811.

"Leaving" Oxford English Dictionary. Second edition. James. A. H. Murray, et.al. Volume VIII. Interval-Looie. Oxford: Clarendon Press. 1989. pp.776-781.

Lorde, Audre. *Sister Outsider*: Essays and Speeches. Trumansberg NY: Crossing Press 1984.

Martindale, Lori. *On Leaving: Poetry, Daesthetics, Timelessness*. Atropos Press. 2014.

Obblink Dirk. 'Two New Poems From Sappho', Zeitschrift für Papyrologie und Epigraphik 189 (2014) 32–49.

Ptolemy, 2nd century. Ptolemy's Almagest. London: Duckworth. 1984

Ronell, Avital. Lecture. EGS. 2009; 2010; 2013.
Ronell, Avital. *Crack Wars*. University of Nebraska Press. 1992.

———. *Fighting Theory*. In Conversation with Anne Dufourmanetelle. Trans. Catherine Porter. Urbana, Chicago, Springfield: University of Illinois. 2010.

——— *Finitude's Score*: Essays for the End of the Millenium. Lincoln Nebraska: University of Nebraska Press, 1994.

———. *Stupidity*. Chicago: University of Illinois Press, 2002.

_____. *The Test Drive.* Urbana: University of Illinois Press, 2005.

_____. *The Telephone Book.* University of Nebraska Press: Lincoln. 1991.

_____. *The ÜberReader.* Ed. Diane Davis. Urbaba and Chicago: University of Illinois Press. 2008.

Sappho. Fragments. Sappho, and Aaron Poochigian. *Stung with*

Love: Poems and Fragments. London: Penguin Books, 2009. Print. P.87.

Sappho. "To One who Loved not Poetry." Trans. Edwin Arnold. *Greek Poets in English Verse*, ed. William Hyde Appleton. Cambridge: Riverside Press, 1893.

Sappho, and Anne Carson. *If Not, Winter*. Poems of Sappho, 2002.

Schirmacher, Wolfgang. "What If? A Tribute to Jacques Derrida."

Poiesis: A Journal of the Arts and Communication. 2005. Pp. 6-9.

Scholasticus, Socrates: The Murder of Hypatia (late 4th century). From *Ecclesiastical History*. Book VI. Ch. 15.

Simkin, John (January 2016). "Sophie Scholl" Spartacus Educational. Retrieved September 8, 2020.

"Timeless" Oxford English Dictionary. Second edition. James.

A. H. Murray, et.al. Volume XVII u-Thrivingly. Oxford: Clarendon Press. 1989. pp.100-114.

van Oosterwijck, Maria. *Vanitas with Sunflower and Jewelry Box*, c. 1665, Public Domain.

van Oosterwijck, Maria. *Vanitas-Still Life*, 1668, Kunsthistorisches Museum. Public Domain.

Vallant, Wallerant. Portrait of Maria van

Oosterwijck (1630-93); *Flower Painter*; 1671. Public Domain.

Zucchi, Antonio. 1773. "Catullus Comforting Lesbia over the Death of Her Pet Sparrow and Writing an Ode." Wikipedia Commons Public Domain.

List of Images:

> Cover:
> Still life of flowers, 1669 (oil on canvas), Oosterwyck, Maria van (1630-93)
> / Cincinnati Art Museum, Ohio,
> USA / © Cincinnati Art Museum / Bequest of Mrs. L.W. Scott Alter / Bridgeman Images
>
> Image 1 (p. 40):
> Sheet Music.
>
> Image 2 (p. 44):
> Fragment of a poem

on Sappho's brother Charaxus, 3rd century C.E. Papyrus 739. Public Domain.

Image 3 (p. 54): Sappho; the Brygos Painter, from 470 B.C. Public Domain.

Image 4 (p. 77): *Sappho Kissing Her Lyre*. Jules-Élie Delaunay. Public Domain.

Image 5 (p. 82): Zucchi, Antonio. 1773. "Catullus Comforting Lesbia over the Death of Her Pet Sparrow and Writing an Ode." Wikipedia Commons Public Domain.

Image 6 (p. 155): Photograph: Unknown. Actress of the play Hypatia. Possibly Mary Anderson, circa 1900. Hypatia b. Public Domain.

Image 7 (p. 157): By Fastfission - From Edward Grant, "Celestial Orbs in the Latin Middle Ages", Isis, Vol. 78, No. 2. (Jun., 1987), pp. 152-173. See also: F. A. C. Mantello and A. G. Rigg, "Medieval Latin: An Introduction and Bibliographical Guide", The Catholic University of America Press, p. 365 (on-line text here)., Public Domain, https://commons.wikimedia.org/w/index.php?curid=317560

Image 8 (p. 181): Raphael *School of Athens*. Public Domain.

Image 9: *Gentileschi, Artemisia. Judith Slaying Holofernes* (1614–20) Original Oil on canvas 199 x 162 cm Galleria degli Uffizi, Florence. Room 90. By Permission of the Uffizi Ministry of Culture. Warning of further duplications and reproductions.

Image 9 (p. 190): *Gentileschi, Artemisia. Judith Slaying Holofernes* (1614–20) Public Domain Image: Wiki Commons.

Image 10 (p. 192): Artemisia Gentileschi. *In Judith and her Maidservant*, Image: (Free Public Domain) Wiki commons.

Image 11 (p. 195): Artemisia Gentileschi. Self Portrait as an

Allegory of Painting (La Pittura). 1638-39. Public Domain.

Image 12 (p. 199): Artemisia Gentileschi's *Sleeping Venus*. Circa. 1625-1630.

Image 13 (p. 209): Two Satyrs and a Maenad. Greek Red Figure. 380-370. Louvre, Paris. Public Domain. By Adolphseck Painter - User: Bibi Saint-Pol, own work, 2007-07-21, Public Domain, https://commons.wikimedia.org/w/index.php?curid=2454918

Image 14 (p. 213): Dieric Bouts "Hell" or "Fall of the Damned" (circa 1420-1475) [Public domain].

Image 15 (p. 215): By Unknown author - Extract of Codex Magliabechiano (cf. FAMSI (Foundation for the Advancement of Mesoamerican

Studies, Inc.), Public Domain, https://commons.wikimedia.org/w/index.php?curid=7828418

Image 16 (p. 217): Mictēcacihuātl, Aztec. Lady of the Dead, Skeletal Aztec goddess of death. Codex Borgia. Unknown author, Public domain, via Wikimedia Commons.

Image 17 (p. 219): Our Lady Death. Muerte-Blanca. [Public domain].

The Little Book of *Daesthetics* |425

Image 18 (p. 229): Jan de Heem's "Still Life with Lobster" (1643). Oil. Public Domain.

Image 19 (p. 236): The Novgorod Codex. Public Domain.

Image 20 (p. 239): Roman Mosaic of the wheel of fortune. 1st century BC. Public Domain.

Image 21 & 22 (p. 241, p. 244): Death and the

Maiden (1518-1520) by Hans Baldung Grien.

Image 23 (p. 253): Portrait of Maria van Oosterwijck (1630-93); *Flower Painter*; Wallerant Vallant. 1671.

Image 24 (p. 256): Maria van Oosterwijck *Vanitas with Sunflower and Jewelry Box*, c. 1665. Public Domain.

Image 25 (p. 259): Maria van

Oosterwijck's *Vanitas-Still Life*, 1668, Kunsthistorisches Museum. Public Domain.

Image 26 (p. 264): Kali Trampling Shiva. By Raja Ravi Varma - http://images.wellcome.ac.uk/indexplus/obf_images/06/be/c9c466b8dd2eca222a98d0a1e171.jpg, Public Domain, https://commons.wikimedia.org/w/index.php?curid=21792915

Image 27 (p. 266): Sandro Botticelli, *The Birth of Venus* (c.1486). Uffizi, Florence. By Sandro Botticelli – By Permission of the Ministry of Culture. Adjusted levels from File: Sandro Botticelli - La nascita di Venere - Google Art Project.jpg, originally from Google Art Project. Compression Photoshop level 9., Public Domain, https://commons.wikimedia.org/w/index.php?curid=22507491

Image 28 (p. 273): Vanitas Still Life with Portrait. By Pieter Claesz
1628 - anagoria, Public Domain, https://commons.wikimedia.org/w/index.php?curid=26404351

Image 29 (p. 299): text: caesura mark

Image 30 (p. 303): music note. PD.

Image 31 (p. 304): sheet music. PD.

Image 32 (p. 305): Blank Sheet Music PD

Image 33 (p. 319): Sheet Music. PD. Image 33: Fragment. Public Domain. Wikicommons

Image 34 (p. 377): Moth eating paper. Natural History Print. 1840.

The Little Book of Daesthetics is a fragmented dictionary on the word daesthetics. The little book goes into philosophy and the lacunae in archives, fragments of poetry, and other arts, such as painting and music.

/deTH/. The state of being dead.

The little book goes into philosophy and the lacunae in archives, fragments of poetry, and other arts, such as painting and music.

d/es THedik/ a philosophy of art.

About the Author:

Dr. Lori Martindale is a Washington based writer and artist.

www.ingramcontent.com/pod-product-compliance
Lightning Source LLC
Chambersburg PA
CBHW062020290426
44108CB00024B/2725